THE

EVERYTHING KIDS'®

Christmas Puzzle & Activity Book

Hours of holiday fun!

Beth L. Blair & Jennifer A. Ericsson

Adams Media Corporation
Avon, Massachusetts

Merry Christmas, Virginia. With love, Jenny and Beth

EDITORIAL
Publishing Director: Gary M. Krebs
Managing Editor: Kate McBride
Copy Chief: Laura MacLaughlin
Acquisitions Editor: Bethany Brown
Development Editor: Julie Gutin
Production Editor: Khrysti Nazzaro

PRODUCTION
Production Director: Susan Beale
Production Manager: Michelle Roy Kelly
Series Designer: Colleen Cunningham
Layout and Graphics: Paul Beatrice,
Colleen Cunningham, Rachael Eiben,
Daria Perreault, Erin Ring, Frank Rivera

Published by Adams Media, an F+W Publications Company
57 Littlefield Street, Avon, MA 02322 U.S.A.
www.adamsmedia.com

ISBN: 1-58062-965-2

Printed in the United States of America.

J   I   H   G   F   E   D   C   B

Cover illustrations by Dana Regan.
Interior illustrations by Kurt Dolber.
Puzzles by Beth Blair.

Puzzle Power Software by Centron Software Technologies, Inc. was used to create puzzle grids.

Contents

Introduction

Christmas is a magical time of the year. We are filled with excitement and anticipation of all the fun times we will have. There is a sense of wonder in the air, and we're busy with special activities we do only once a year—trimming the tree, baking Christmas cookies, wrapping numerous gifts, building a gingerbread house.

We've created *The Everything® Kids' Christmas Puzzle & Activity Book* as another way to celebrate the season. Included are all kinds of puzzles for all kinds of kids. This book is more stuffed than a Christmas stocking, and just as much fun to open! There are word searches and mazes, rebuses and codes, picture puzzles and math puzzles.

We suggest you pick up this book when you need a quiet time during the hectic Christmas season. Maybe you just got back from the mall. Maybe you just helped to clean the house. Maybe you just shoveled the driveway! Whatever the reason, sit down, relax—and do some puzzles.

To get you in the mood, **see if you can find seven synonyms (words that are similar) to Q-U-I-E-T hidden in this word search:**

We're sure this book will add even more joy to your holiday season—Merry Christmas!

```
N P E A C E F U L
T O S Q U I T V H
R G I H U S H E D
A F L S R S W H I
N E E P E C A L M
Q D N X O L E F J
U C T A B N E G K
I B Y Z C D M S L
L A S E R E N E S
```

Beth L. Blair   *Jennifer A. Ericsson*

Chapter 1

Around the World

Ancient Origins

The ancient Romans held a celebration in late December honoring Saturn, the god of agriculture. They decorated their homes, lit candles, sang, and even exchanged gifts of cake and fruit. This pre-Christmas holiday was called Saturnalia. How many three-letter words (or longer) can you make from these letters? Try to make 20. Give yourself a big **HO-HO-HO** if you can find a five- or a seven-letter word!

SATURNALIA

1. _____
2. _____
3. _____
4. _____
5. _____
6. _____
7. _____
8. _____
9. _____
10. _____
11. _____
12. _____
13. _____
14. _____
15. _____
16. _____
17. _____
18. _____
19. _____
20. _____

Pucker Up

In many countries, including the United States, people hang a certain plant over their doorways at Christmastime. Originally used to ward off evil spirits, it is now seen as a symbol of Christmas joy. To find out the name of this plant, make a three-letter word on each line by placing a letter in the empty middle box. When you're finished, read down the shaded column. If you ever find yourself standing under this plant, expect a friendly kiss!

I		P
S	I	T
A		K
I	T	S
O		D
P		G
A		E
W		N
L	E	D

To Market, to Market

Germany is very famous for its Christmas markets, where shoppers can buy holiday food, toys, and decorations. Below you will see the name of the most popular of these markets. Can you guess the English translation of this name?

CHRISTKINDESMARKT

Christmas Greetings

Listed below are some of the many ways "Merry Christmas" can be said in other languages. Can you fit them all into the grid? We've left you some **G-R-E-E-T-I-N-G-S** to get you started.

Nollaigshonadhuit

Feliz Navidad

Joyeux Noel

Frohliche Weihnachten

Buon Natale

God Jul

Mboni Chrismen

Boas Festas

Chuc Mung Giang Sinh

Cestitamo Bozic

Want to know where each of these greetings is said? When you've filled in the puzzle, match the number for each greeting to one of the countries listed below.

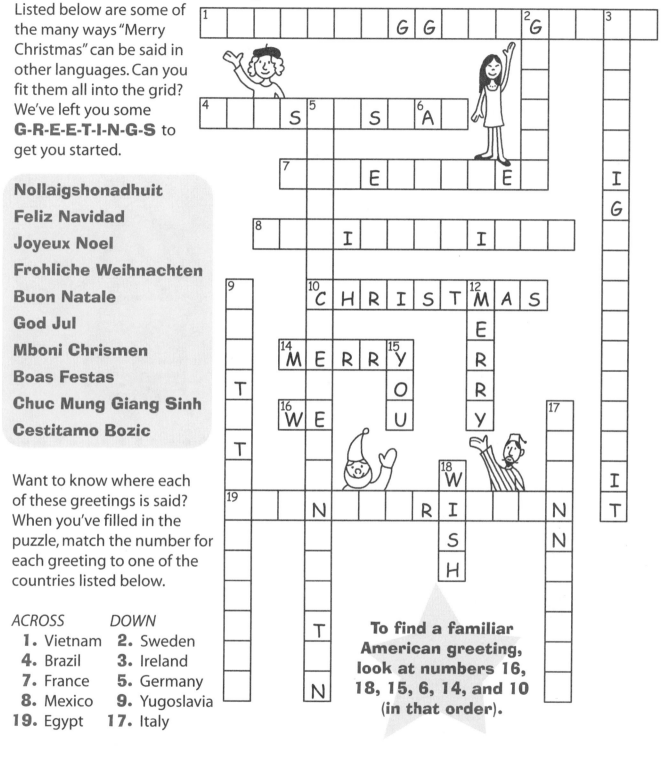

To find a familiar American greeting, look at numbers 16, 18, 15, 6, 14, and 10 (in that order).

ACROSS
1. Vietnam
4. Brazil
7. France
8. Mexico
19. Egypt

DOWN
2. Sweden
3. Ireland
5. Germany
9. Yugoslavia
17. Italy

Gift-Giver

Here in the United States, Santa Claus brings presents on Christmas morning. Around the world, this special person is called by different names. Cross out the letters **S-A-N-T-A C-L-A-U-S** in each of the lines below. Read the remaining letters to learn the name of five international gift-givers. **SPECIAL DIRECTIONS:** Cross out the letters *in order* from left to right. Cross out each letter only as many times as it appears in the name SANTA CLAUS. For example, you will cross out two *S*s, but only one T.

SFANATTHAER CCHRLISATUMASS

_____

SPAENRTEA CNLOAEULS

_____

SANLTAA CBLEFAAUNSA

_____

SKANRTIAS KRCILNAUGLSE

_____

SBAANTBAOCULSHAKUSA

_____

Nice Neighbor

Do you know what product Canada sends south to help bring the joy of Christmas to the United States?

To find out, use a simple number substitution code (A=1, B=2, etc.)

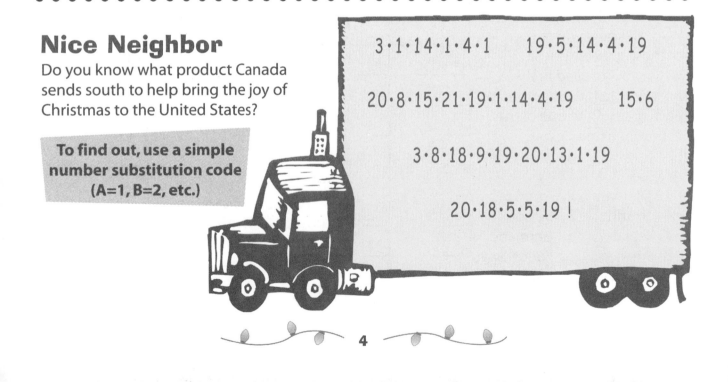

3·1·14·1·4·1   19·5·14·4·19

20·8·15·21·19·1·14·4·19   15·6

3·8·18·9·19·20·13·1·19

20·18·5·5·19 !

The 12 Days of Christmas

Not all countries have big Christmas celebrations on December 25. Many world festivities occur on the days between December 25 and January 6. "The 12 Days of Christmas" is a popular Christmas carol that lists all the presents given to a young lady by her true love during this time.

Use the picture clues to figure out all the gifts the young lady received!

Hidden Angels

Angels are popular with holiday shoppers the world over. Can you find the 11 angels hidden in this busy market?

What's Xmas?

The letter X stands for the Greek letter *chi*. Chi is the first letter in the Greek word for *Christ*. Over time, the letter X came to stand for the name of Christ. That's why some people write *Xmas* instead of *Christmas*!

Can you find your way through this giant Xmas from **START** to **END**?

START

END

Fill It Up!

In the United States, we hang stockings on Christmas Eve for Santa to fill. Children in other countries might leave out another item of clothing to be filled with gifts. What is it?

To find out, unscramble the five words below (all are different things you can wear). When you are done, read the letters in shaded boxes from top to bottom.

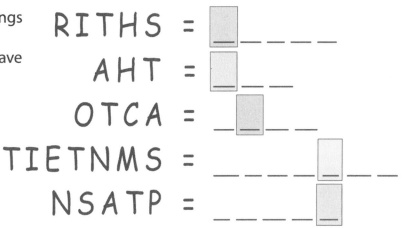

RITHS = _ _ _ _ _

AHT = _ _ _

OTCA = _ _ _ _

TIETNMS = _ _ _ _ _ _ _

NSATP = _ _ _ _ _

Sweet Sweden

For Christmas in Sweden, young girls dress as St. Lucia, the patron saint of light. Connect both sets of dots to get a close look at this beautiful costume. The two number 1s are circled for you.

When you are finished, color the crown in shades of green, and draw St. Lucia a lovely pair of eyes! The candles should stay white.

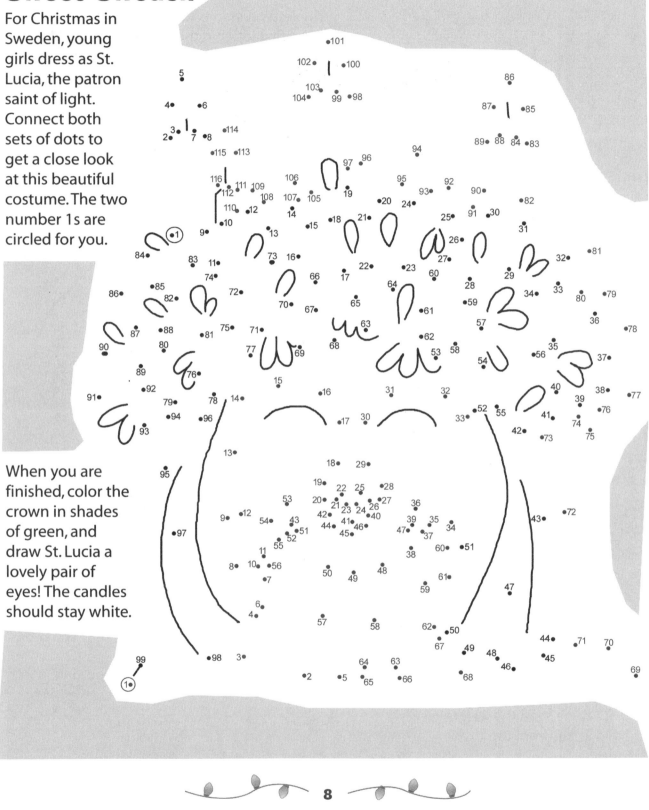

Popular Poppers

In Great Britain, "Christmas crackers" are a special holiday treat. These paper-covered tubes have small toys hidden inside and make a popping or cracking noise when the ends are pulled. Read the clues below and see if you can complete the words or phrases that all contain the letters **P-O-P**. When you're finished, decorate these crackers with bright colors, stripes, and stars. Make each one different!

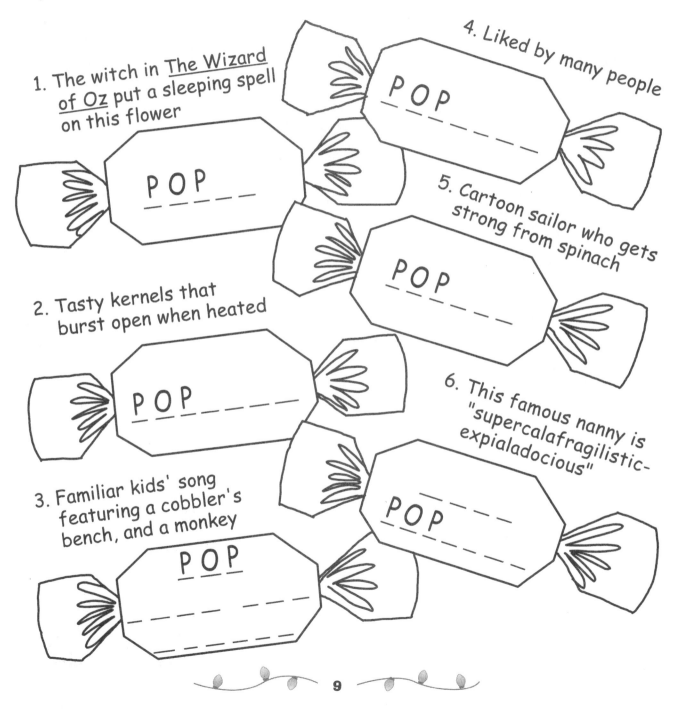

1. The witch in <u>The Wizard of Oz</u> put a sleeping spell on this flower

P O P _ _ _

2. Tasty kernels that burst open when heated

P O P _ _ _ _

3. Familiar kids' song featuring a cobbler's bench, and a monkey

P O P _ _ _ _ _ _ _ _ _

4. Liked by many people

P O P _ _ _ _ _

5. Cartoon sailor who gets strong from spinach

P O P _ _ _ _

6. This famous nanny is "supercalafragilistic-expialadocious"

_ _ _ _ P O P _ _ _

Greek Greetings

Greece is a country with miles of coastland and many fishermen. For Christmas, their small fishing boats are decorated with shining lights. What color are these lights? To find out, answer each question below and put the letters into their proper place in the grid. Work back and forth until you have the answer.

1 F	2 J	3 B	4 I		5 E	6 G	7 A C	8 C	9 H	10 G	11 D	12 G
	13 G	14 A H	15 K	16 A I	17 K		18 E	19 D	20 K	21 K	22 G	
23 D	24 E	25 K	26 C		27 H	28 A L	29 E	30 I		31 H	32 H	33 A D
	34 B	35 I	36 J	37 B	38 F		39 E	40 B	41 C	42 B	43 F	44 F

A. A young boy or girl
C̲ H̲ I̲ L̲ D̲
7 14 16 28 33

B. The color of snow
___ ___ ___ ___ ___
34 42 40 37 3

C. A fully grown pig
___ ___ ___
26 8 41

D. The number after one
___ ___ ___
11 23 19

E. Put together piece by piece
___ ___ ___ ___ ___
18 29 24 39 5

F. Try something new
___ ___ ___ ___
43 38 44 1

G. To annoy playfully
___ ___ ___ ___ ___
13 6 10 22 12

H. Building where farm animals live
___ ___ ___ ___
27 31 9 32

I. A word used to call someone
___ ___ ___
35 30 4

J. Short way of saying hello
___ ___
2 36

K. A special sweet snack
___ ___ ___ ___ ___
21 17 15 20 25

			B
B	B		W
			B
			W
B	B		B
			W
			B
			W
			B

HINT: The colored Christmas lights on Greek boats are the same as those used in the Greek flag! Here is a flag for you to color. Break the code to see where each color goes.

10

Warm Wishes

Holiday greetings are arriving at your house from all over the world. Look carefully at each card, and see if you can match each one to the person who sent it! Write the correct number next to the card.

1. Man Po, China

2. Juan, Mexico

3. Fawn, Alaska

4. Dave, Australia

5. Abi, Ethiopia

6. Mathilde, France

Favorite Flower

A traditional Christmas decoration that we enjoy in the United States originally came from Mexico. There, it is called the "Flower of the Holy Night." Break the code and fill the correct letters into the shaded boxes. When you are finished, you will know the more familiar name for this beautiful red, pink, or white plant.

two after N

four before S

one before J

four after J

between R and T

the fifth one

three after Q

two before V

between H and J

the first one

Pretty Parols

Lanterns called "parols," or Christmas stars, are very popular in the Philippines. Some communities even have contests to decide which parol is the best. While all of the parols on this page are beautiful, only two are exactly alike. Can you find and circle them?

Chapter 2

Piles of Presents

Wishful Thinking

Here are the Johnson family's Christmas wish lists. Can you figure out what each family member secretly wants?

Mom

sweateR
gardening tOols
watCh
pasta maKer
slippErs
stationeRy

DAD

Crosswords

bAthrobe
country Music
dEnim shirt
gRill

baseball cAp

Meagan

teen Magazines
cd plAyer
mini-sKirt
baskEtball
blUe jeans
movie Pass

TiMMY

maGic tricks
long Underwear
comIc books
jackeT
sneAkers
skateboaRd

DoRA

diapeRs
blAnket
Teddy bear
sTroller
mobiLe
baby powdEr

Pepper

bisCuits
chew tOy
balL
bowL
leAsh
keRchief

Bow Tie

Kayla can do a nifty Christmas trick. She can pick up a piece of ribbon using both hands and tie it in a knot without letting go of either end of the ribbon! Can you figure out how she is able to do it?

Who Gets What?

Two fathers and two sons have unwrapped three gifts. Each of them has exactly one present. How can this be? To find out, answer as many clues below as you can, and fill the letters you have into the grid. Work back and forth between the box and the clues until you figure it out.

1 H	2 C	3 G	4 E		5 E	6 D	7 B				
8 G	9 G	10 G	11 C	12 C	13 A F	14 H	15 B	16 D	17 F	18 A R
19 A F	20 D	21 F	22 E	23 A E	24 B		25 C	26 H	27 G	
28 B	29 A O	30 F								

A. To show a desire to do something

$\underset{29}{O}\ \underset{13}{F}\ \underset{19}{F}\ \underset{23}{E}\ \underset{18}{R}$

B. To stop working

$\overline{24}\ \overline{7}\ \overline{28}\ \overline{15}$

C. Your fingers are part of this

$\overline{2}\ \overline{25}\ \overline{11}\ \overline{12}$

D. A cheerleader's cheer

$\overline{6}\ \overline{20}\ \overline{16}$

E. Dried grass for horses

$\overline{22}\ \overline{5}\ \overline{4}$

F. The number after nine

$\overline{21}\ \overline{17}\ \overline{30}$

G. The year you are in school

$\overline{8}\ \overline{9}\ \overline{10}\ \overline{27}\ \overline{3}$

H. A light brown color

$\overline{1}\ \overline{14}\ \overline{26}$

Squiggle Giggles

What gift could be inside each of the boxes below?
Use the lines in each box to help create a pile of presents!

Pretty Packages

Which two presents are exactly the same?

Giving Gifts

You probably want to give a present to many people at Christmastime. Read the clues carefully and see how many of them you can fit into the crossword grid. We left you some **G-I-F-T-S** to get you started.

ACROSS

2. People who are related to you
5. Person who checks out books for you
6. Person who helps you learn
8. People who live near you

DOWN

1. Person who is the head of your church
3. Person who brings you letters and packages
4. Person who you like
7. Person who helps you in sports

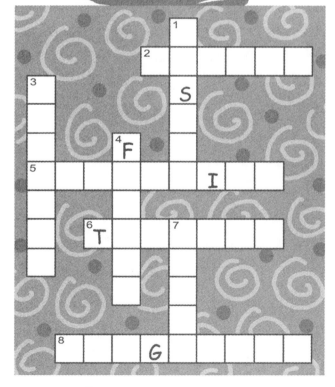

Picking the Perfect Present

Brian has saved up $20 to spend on Christmas presents for three friends. Alex likes sports, Jason likes animals, and Allison likes crafts. Brian chose one item for each friend from the store on the next page, and spent exactly $20. Can you figure out what item he bought for each friend?

HINT: First fill in the list below with all the items in the store that each friend might like.

Alex
(sports)

Jason
(animals)

Allison
(crafts)

Missing Package

Kelly did a lot of Christmas shopping at the mall. But she dropped one of her packages! Can you help Santa's elf return it to her?

Presents Hink Pinks

The answers to Hink Pinks are two rhyming words with the same number of syllables. See if you can figure these out.

1. What do you call a present that arrives very quickly?

   _ _ _ _ _ _   _ _ _ _ _

2. What do you have when you accidentally break two presents?

   _ _ _ _ _ _ _   _ _ _ _ _ _ _

3. What do you see when your brother opens the perfect present?

   _ _ _   _ _ _

4. What do you call the light that shines off the looped ribbon on top of a present?

   _ _ _   _ _ _ _

5. What do you call it when you cut the wrapping paper the wrong way?

   _ _ _ _ _   _ _ _ _

6. What do you call a kid who rips open all the presents on Christmas morning?

   _ _ _ _ _   _ _ _ _ _ _

7. What do you call a nice gift?

   _ _ _ _ _ _ _ _ _

Wacky Word

Who brings presents to cats and dogs on Christmas? To find the answer, color in the letters **F-L-U-F-F-Y** and **R-O-V-E-R** in the grid below. Read the remaining letters.

F L R S U O
A F N R V
F T V E Y R
R A O V U
P F V L A E
U W F F L
R F S Y R O

Gift Tags

Eight girlfriends had a holiday party and each brought a gift for one of the other girls. On each tag is written a group of similar words. Use these clues to figure out the names of all the girls. The first one has been done for you.

wren
blue jay
chickadee
sparrow
to: ROBIN

October
March
August
January
to:

hope trust
to:
kindness peace

Ohio
Vermont Maine
Missouri
to:

diamond
topaz
emerald
sapphire
to:

lavender
magenta
red indigo
to:

marigold
daisy tulip
carnation
to:

All Wrapped Up

Drew just got a great guitar from his grandma. Before he opens the package, can you tell which guitar he got?

to Drew ♥ Grams

Where Are the Presents?

Clever Santa has hidden all the presents! Can you find the following 10 toys in this picture? BOOK, TRAIN, AIRPLANE, CRAYONS, JUMP ROPE, SKATEBOARD, ROLLER SKATE, BASEBALL, SCISSORS, PAINTBRUSH.

Chapter 3

Deck the Hall

Oh, Christmas Tree

Replace each ornament with the correct letter and you will discover which country is believed to have put up the first Christmas tree.

A = gingerbread man
D = bird
E = heart
G = angel
H = snowman
I = candy cane
M = candle
N = stocking
O = snowflake
R = horn
S = bow
T = star
Y = present

Ornament Scramble

Take the letters in each ornament, add one missing letter, then unscramble them to discover the name of six old-fashioned tree decorations. The missing letters read from top to bottom to spell out the name of a unique ornament with a fun tradition. The first person to find this ornament on Christmas morning gets an extra gift!

1. _____

2. _____

3. _____

4. _____

5. _____

6. _____

BONUS: _____

The Perfect Tree

Help this family find the perfect tree. How will they know which one? It has a star on top!

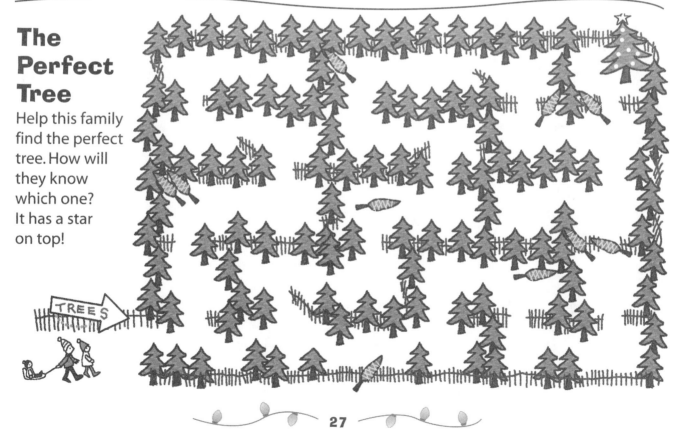

TREES

Which Wreath?

One wreath doesn't belong in this set. Which one and why?

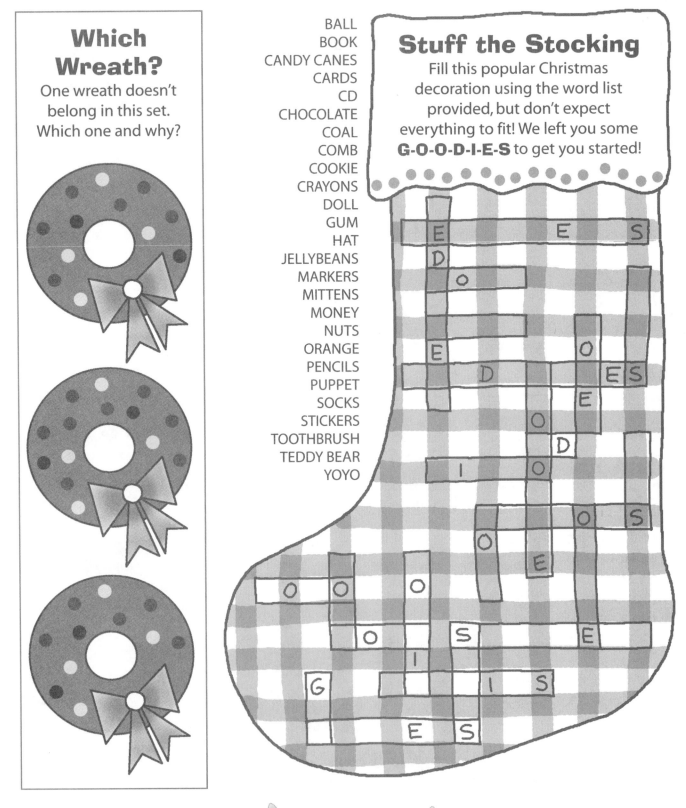

BALL
BOOK
CANDY CANES
CARDS
CD
CHOCOLATE
COAL
COMB
COOKIE
CRAYONS
DOLL
GUM
HAT
JELLYBEANS
MARKERS
MITTENS
MONEY
NUTS
ORANGE
PENCILS
PUPPET
SOCKS
STICKERS
TOOTHBRUSH
TEDDY BEAR
YOYO

Stuff the Stocking

Fill this popular Christmas decoration using the word list provided, but don't expect everything to fit! We left you some **G-O-O-D-I-E-S** to get you started!

String of Lights

Use the clues to fill in the bulbs. The last letter of one word is the first letter of the next.
HINT: Follow the string of lights in order, even if it looks like you're spelling backward!

1. Santa's helper
2. Where there's smoke, there's _____
3. What you hear when you yell down a well
4. What you use to row a boat
5. You could float down a river on this

When you have filled in all the lights, write the letters in the white bulbs on the dotted lines. You will get the answer to this riddle:

What present did the Christmas tree give to his girlfriend?

A __ __ __ __ __ __ __!

How Symbolic

Do you ever see candy canes at Halloween, or Santa at the 4th of July? No way! Over the years, certain symbols have come to represent Christmas. Find these three groups of symbols in the grid.

Group 1

Group 2

Group 3

City Lights

Big Glass Corporation likes to decorate in a big way. Follow the directions to see which offices are part of the decorating plan. Color those windows green, and see what holiday decoration will show up when the lights go on!

HINT: If the numbers are listed with a dash in-between (for example, 5-8), you must color in the 5th window, the 8th window, and all the windows in between!

12th floor:
windows 3, 5-8, 10, 12

11th floor:
windows 3, 5, 8, 10-12

10th floor:
windows 1-3, 5-8, 11

9th floor: no windows

8th floor: windows 6, 7

7th floor: windows 5-8

6th floor: windows 4-9

5th floor: windows 3-10

4th floor: windows 2-11

3rd floor: windows 1-12

2nd floor: windows 6, 7

1st floor: front doors

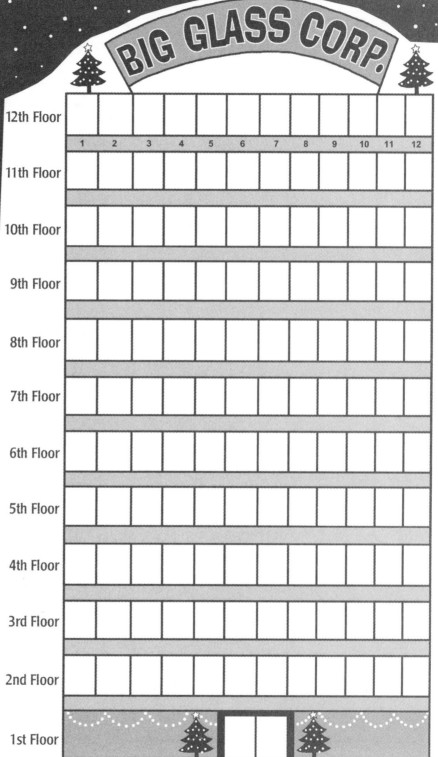

Yard Art

All of the plastic Santas in this neighborhood look very similar. But the one that Carla likes is unique. Can you find it? Carla's Santa has all of the following features:

- ★ 1 pompom on hat
- ★ tall boots
- ★ round nose
- ★ smiling
- ★ long beard
- ★ square belt buckle

Christmas Rings

Solve this puzzle to find out the difference between the ordinary alphabet and the Christmas alphabet. Look carefully at the rings. Some look like they are linked through each other. Others look like two rings that overlap, but are NOT linked. **In the blanks provided underneath, copy down, in order, only the letters you find inside the unlinked rings. The first two have been done for you.**

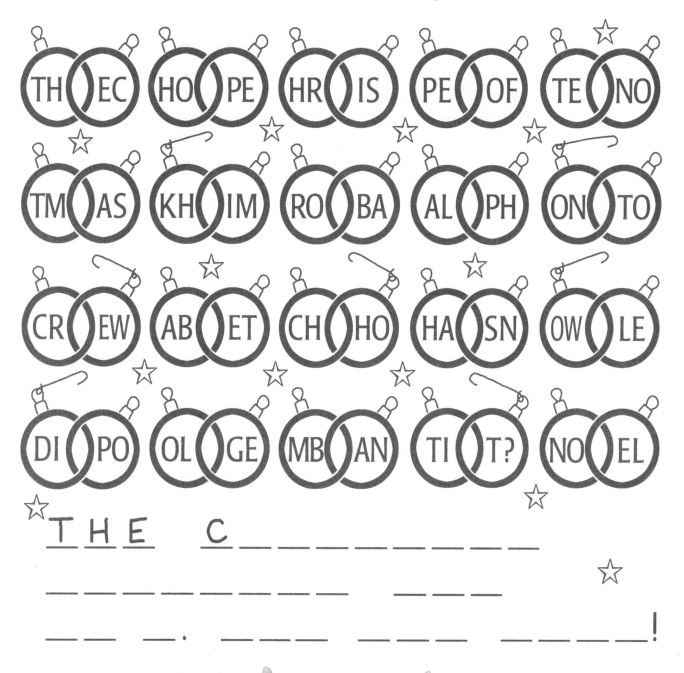

THE C _ _ _ _ _ _ _ _

_ _ _ _ _ _ _ _ _ _ _

_ _ _. _ _ _ _ _ _ _ _ _ _ _ !

Oops!

A Christmas elf has dropped an ornament. Which one of the four trains do you get when you put the pieces together again?

Candles

Figure out where to put the scrambled letters in each candle. They all fit in the spaces directly underneath. When you have them in the correct place, you will know the answer to this riddle:

**Which candle burns longer—
a red one or a green one?**

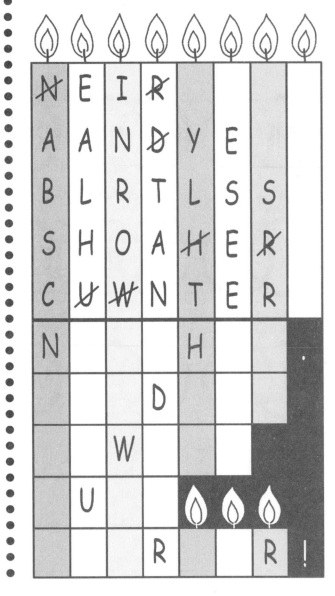

Chapter 4

Christmas Goodies

Getting Groceries

All the items that Mom needs to finish her Christmas baking are written on the shopping list. Can you find all the items in the word search grid on the next page? The words can run top to bottom, side to side, diagonally, and even backward! Cross each word off the list as you find it.

HELPFUL HINT: Instead of circling the words in the grid with a pencil or pen, use a highlighter or light-colored marker and simply run a line through each word. This makes it much easier to see all the letters, especially when words overlap.

EXTRA FUN: Look for all the letter *X*s that appear in the grid. Use a dark-colored marker to highlight each one and you'll get a picture of Mom's favorite treat to bake. Look a little harder, and you will see that all the ingredients for this treat are hidden inside the picture!

Mom's List

ALLSPICE	FLOUR
ALMONDS	GELATIN
BAKING POWDER	GINGER
BAKING SODA	GRAHAM CRACKERS
BANANAS	JIMMIES
BROWN SUGAR	MARSHMALLOWS
BUTTER	MILK
CARAMELS	MOLASSES
CHERRIES	NUTMEG
CHOCOLATE CHIPS	OATMEAL
CINNAMON	OIL
CLOVES	O.J.
COCOA	PEANUT BUTTER
COCONUT	PECANS
CONFECTIONERS'	PEPPERMINT
SUGAR	RAISINS
CRANBERRIES	RUM
CREAM	SALT
CREAM CHEESE	SUGAR
CURRANTS	VANILLA
DATES	WALNUTS
EGGS	

Missing Cake

Wait a minute—Mom baked a Christmas cake, and one piece is already missing! Can you find it for her?

```
G A B B C D E S O F G X X X X B R O W N S U G A R
R H A I V J T K A L X B M L F X S E I R R E H C E
A O N P A U Q R T X S A T N L V X W O I L Y Z B T
H A A B N C D E M X F K G U O I X G K L M N A A T
A O N L I P R Q E X R I S T U U X V W Y M I L K U
M Z A C L A U B A X C N D M R F X G H I K L L I B
C W S U L O M P L S X G T E V X J I M M I E S N T
R O A R A X X X X X B S U G A R X X X X X A P G U
A A A R X B C D E O P O A B R S T U W Y O X I P N
C B L A X C L O V E S D N O W G I N G E R X C O A
K C M N X A B L M N O A P S T E F G A B C X E W E
E C O T N X X X X X O P Q R T S X X X X X N Y D P
R H N S P D A B N X B E T H L I X O S C A M V E E
S O D A T E S R Y X N I C E A P X J E R S A O R N
E C S M O G D T O X F T R H S E X T I E M R E I E
I O T S W G U S T X H T H E A T X L R A I S I N S
R L A P C S T N X E L Y S S T H E X R M E H A T E
R A L E A L O Y X R E S X X A T L X L Y M M I U E
E T S C R M S X E S A X H G X E U R X M O A M N H
B E A A A N D X T L H X A E X T S B X A H L A O C
N C R N M D X T O H X I N L G X T O L X I L V C M
A H N S E W X M I T X H O A H X S S T X C O C O A
R I I T L N O X M X O R C T A N X T X A H W N C E
C P T W S A I T X N T I M I Y M O X E T T S D O R C
C S O M E R A G U S S R E N O I T C E F N O C W C
```

How Many Marshmallows?

Six friends were drinking hot chocolate. On the table was a bowl with 20 marshmallows in it. When the kids were finished, there were no marshmallows left! Using the following clues, figure out how many marshmallows each child took.

1. Jessica and Jennifer took the same number.

2. Joshua took two marshmallows.

3. Justin took two fewer marshmallows than John.

4. John took one more marshmallow than Jessica.

5. Jeremy took three times as many marshmallows as Joshua.

Jessica ___ Jennifer ___ Joshua ___ John ___ Jeremy ___ Justin ___

Santa Snacks
Can you find the 10 **S-N-A-C-K-S** that someone left for Santa?

Sweet Riddle

Hold me one way and I look like the letter J. Turn me over, and I look like a shepherd's crook. What am I?

To find the answer, color all the letter *J*s red. Color all the shepherd's crooks green. Then read the remaining white letters!

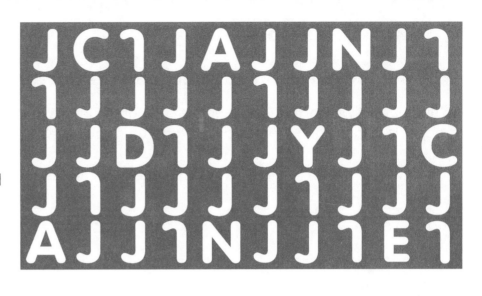

- -

Mmm Mmm . . . Good!

Imagine a plate piled high with all your favorite Christmas goodies, such as cupcakes, sugar cookies, fudge, and more! How can you possibly describe how good everything is? See if you can fit the list of delicious words from top to bottom into the crossword grid. When you are finished, read across the shaded boxes to discover a truly tasty adjective! I left you some of **M-Y B-R-O-W-N-I-E-S** to help out.

EXTRA FUN: Can you use *all* the delicious words in one sentence?

BUTTERY	SPLENDID
CHEWY	SUPER
CREAMY	SWEET
GOOEY	ULTRA
MUNCHY	YUMMY
RICH	

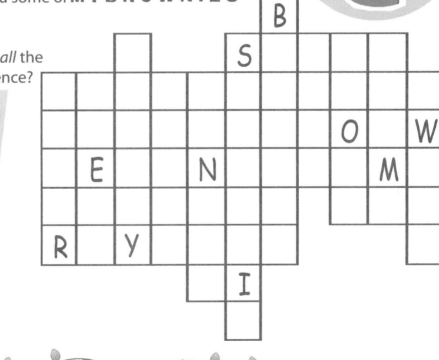

Cookie Questions

Why did the gingerbread man go to the doctor on Christmas Eve?

To find out, answer each question below and put the letters into their proper place in the grid. Work back and forth until you have the answer.

A. Belongs to me

$\underline{\text{M}}$ $\underline{\text{Y}}$
16 18

B. Rounded back part of the foot

$\underline{\quad}$ $\underline{\quad}$ $\underline{\quad}$ $\underline{\quad}$
1 7 8 9

C. Enjoyment

$\underline{\quad}$ $\underline{\quad}$ $\underline{\quad}$
6 15 11

D. Anything against the law

$\underline{\quad}$ $\underline{\quad}$ $\underline{\quad}$ $\underline{\quad}$ $\underline{\quad}$
13 14 10 17 2

E. A happy dog does this with his tail

$\underline{\quad}$ $\underline{\quad}$ $\underline{\quad}$ $\underline{\quad}$
3 4 12 5

1 B	2 D		3 E	4 E	5 E	
6 C	7 B	8 B	9 B	10 D	11 C	12 E
13 D	14 D	15 C	16 A **M**	17 D	18 A **Y**	!

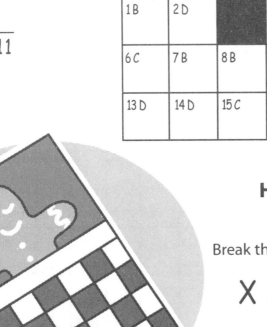

How does a gingerbread man make his bed?

Break this substitution code to find the answer!

X J U I   D P P L J F

$\underline{\quad}$ $\underline{\quad}$ $\underline{\quad}$ $\underline{\quad}$ $\underline{\quad}$ $\underline{\quad}$ $\underline{\quad}$ $\underline{\quad}$ $\underline{\quad}$ $\underline{\quad}$

T I F F U T

$\underline{\quad}$ $\underline{\quad}$ $\underline{\quad}$ $\underline{\quad}$ $\underline{\quad}$ $\underline{\quad}$

Gingerbread Village

Each of the buildings in this gingerbread village is priced at **$20**. But if you buy the trees and snowmen that go with it, the final cost is different. Trees cost **$1.00** and snowmen are **50 cents**. Do a little figuring to find out the total cost of each building with its decorations. Which one is the most expensive?

Look! Good Food

Using the word list provided, can you fill in the blanks of this story with **OO** words? It is okay to use a word more than once.

BOOK	COOL	MOOD	TOOK
GOOD	DOOR	NOON	ZOOM
COOK	LOOK	SOON	

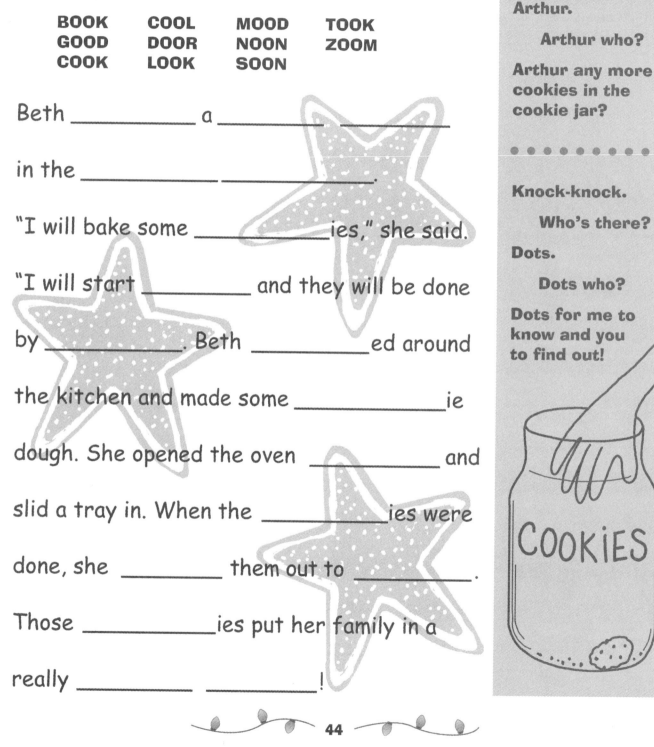

Beth _____ a _____ _____

in the _____ _____.

"I will bake some _____ies," she said.

"I will start _____ and they will be done

by _____. Beth _____ed around

the kitchen and made some _____ie

dough. She opened the oven _____ and

slid a tray in. When the _____ies were

done, she _____ them out to _____.

Those _____ies put her family in a

really _____ _____!

Knock-knock.

Who's there?

Arthur.

Arthur who?

Arthur any more cookies in the cookie jar?

• • • • • • • • • •

Knock-knock.

Who's there?

Dots.

Dots who?

Dots for me to know and you to find out!

COOKIES

44

Cookie Dough

The baked cookies on the cooling rack all came from one of these rolled-out batches of dough. Which one?

Look Alikes

Can you find the identical twin gingerbread boys?

Mixed Mints

Can you find the two swirly mints that are different from the rest?

Tasty Treats

Some of these recipes are missing important ingredients!
Fill in the blanks using words from the bottom of the page.

White and Red Garlands

popped _____,

raw _____,

needle, heavy _____

Crunchy Fudge

_____ chips,

chopped _____, salt,

condensed milk, vanilla

Fruitcake

flour, sugar, baking powder,

salt, eggs, vanilla, dates,

candied _____,

dried _____

Gingerbread Men

butter, sugar, flour, baking soda,

nutmeg, _____, salt,

_____,

_____ cutters

Cheesecake

_____ cracker crumbs,

sugar, butter, eggs, vanilla,

_____,

sour _____

Apple Pie

pastry _____, sugar,

flour, green _____, butter

APPLES   NUTS   MOLASSES   GINGER   CRANBERRIES   CORN

CRUSTS   CHERRIES

COOKIE   THREAD

CREAM   CREAM CHEESE   APRICOTS   GRAHAM   CHOCOLATE

Knock-knock.

Who's there?

Henrietta.

Henrietta who?

Henrietta big bowl of ice cream!

• • • • • • • • • •

Knock-knock.

Who's there?

Ivana.

Ivana who?

Ivana eat a big bowl of ice cream, too!

Santa Sundae

Find your way from bottom to top through Santa's favorite Christmas dessert!

END

START

Chapter 5

Holy Christmas

The Story Behind Christmas

It's important to remember that Christmas is not just about Santa Claus! To find out the deeper meaning of Christmas, cross out the following kinds of words, and read the leftover words from left to right, and top to bottom.

- **Words that rhyme with STAR**
- **Two-letter words starting with A**
- **Words that start with TR**
- **Four-letter words starting with B**

BEST	CHRISTMAS	TREE	IS	BAKE
A	AN	HOLIDAY	TRUST	INTENDED
TRY	TROUBLE	AX	BATH	TRUMPET
AS	TO	TRAP	CELEBRATE	AT
THE	TRAVEL	BIRTH	FAR	OF
TREASURE	JESUS	JAR	CHRIST	CAR

• •

For Goodness' Sake

The true spirit of Christmas is not about being good so Santa will bring you lots of presents. The real rewards are some of the other feelings you can experience at this time of year. Can you figure out what they might be from the picture puzzles below?

1. **1** + DER

2. FR + GOODBYE! + 🚢

3. C + 🌴 − P

4. 🧤 − G

5. 🫛

No Room at the Inn

The story of Christmas tells us that Mary and Joseph traveled to the town of Bethlehem. When they got there, the hotels and inns were all full. Can you help the tired Joseph find the stable where they will spend the night? Walk carefully—Joseph must travel to every inn, but never cross over his own path!

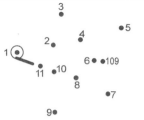

3

2 4 •5

1 ⊙ 6 •109

11 •10 8

•7

9•

Away in a Manger
Connect the dots to form the building in which many people believe the baby Jesus was born. Color the picture when you are done!

12

108

13 •14 69 70 106 107

65

68

66 64 •63

67 71•

15 23 76

17 19 21 72

22 •61 77• 75• 73 104 •105

•16 18 20 •60 78• 103

33 32 24 79• 74 102 101

31

80• •87

26 86 •88

29 25 85

30 27 81• 84 89•

28 •59 82 83 99

100

35 46 47 •58

34 90• •98

36• 45• 48• •57 91• •97

37• 49 92• •96

44• •56

38• 43• 50• •55 93•

39• 42• 51• •54 94• 95

40• •52 •53

41

Christmas Animals
Read across each line and cross out the names of animals that might have been in the stable when Jesus was born. When you are finished, collect the leftover letters from left to right and top to bottom. Write them, in order, in the blanks to discover the name of the animal that carried tired Mary to the stable.

D O X E N O N
N S H E E P
G O A T S K
E Y C O W S

___ ___ ___ ___ ___ ___

Three Kings

Three kings followed a star to Bethlehem so that they could honor the baby Jesus. Use the crown decoder to spell out the names of these three important visitors.

A B C D E F G H I K

L M N O P R S T Y Z

————————————————— ,

——————————————— ,

and ———————————

BONUS: Use the same decoder to figure out what gifts the kings brought.

——————— , ——————————, and

————————————————————

53

Good Tidings of Great Joy

Part of the Christmas story tells of how an angel appeared to a special group of people, telling them about the birth of Christ. Follow these directions and you will see to whom the angel appeared.

Color the picture when you're done!

1. Find box 1-A and copy it into square 1-A in the grid.
2. Find box 1-B and copy it into square 1-B in the grid.
3. Continue this process until you've copied all the boxes in the grid.

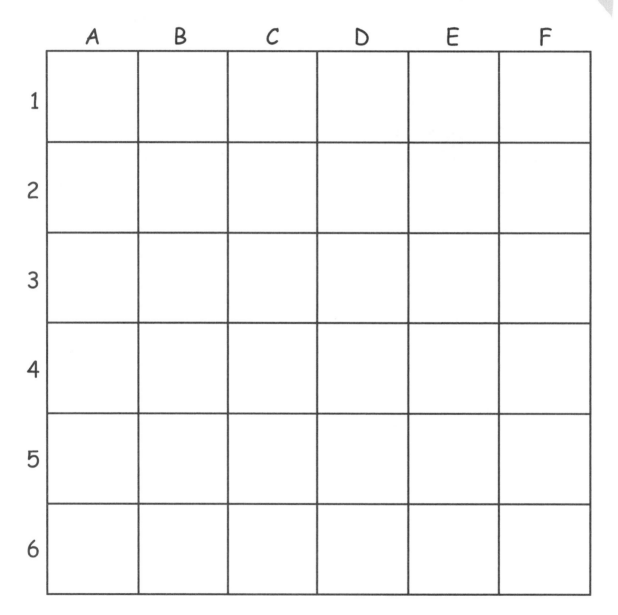

3D   3E   4E   1D   5B   2D

2A   4C   2E   6C   5C   6F

5D   1C   3C   3B   5E   6A

4A   1E   6D   1B   5A   2B

3F   2C   2F   6E   1A   3A

5F   6B   4D   1F   4B   4F

Where's the Star?

It's not always easy to follow a star in the sky! See if you can find the star hiding in this night sky.

Christmas Story

Fit all of these words from the story of Christmas into the grid.

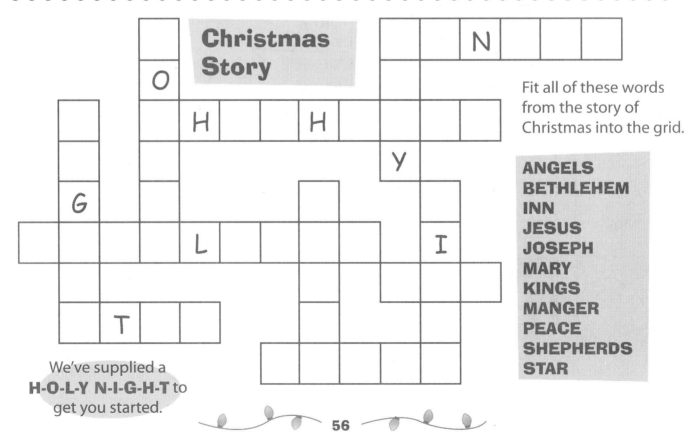

ANGELS
BETHLEHEM
INN
JESUS
JOSEPH
MARY
KINGS
MANGER
PEACE
SHEPHERDS
STAR

We've supplied a **H-O-L-Y N-I-G-H-T** to get you started.

Advent Calendar

The season of Advent is a special time in certain churches. It lasts from the end of November until Christmas Day. Many people enjoy using an Advent calendar to count down the days until Christmas. Each day, a small door is opened on the calendar and a holiday picture is revealed. See if you can figure out what is hidden behind each of these doors by the three letters you can see for each day. A word list is provided so you can match the letters to a word. **HINT:** Some words can fit behind more than one door, but there's only one way that uses all the words.

AND Day 1	**SET** Day 2	**ELL** Day 3	**PRE** Day 4
NAM Day 5	**IGH** Day 6	**LAM** Day 7	**NDY** Day 8
ORN Day 9	**HOL** Day 10	**CRA** Day 11	**WFL** Day 12
OOK Day 13	**RCH** Day 14	**BIR** Day 15	**REA** Day 16
TOC Day 17	**MEL** Day 18	**CRO** Day 19	**ROL** Day 20
DRU Day 21	**STA** Day 22	**NGE** Day 23	**TIV** Day 24

ANGEL
BELLS
BIRD
CANDLE
CANDY CANE
CAMEL
CAROL
CHURCH
COOKIE
CROWN
DRUM
HOLLY
HORN
LAMB
NATIVITY
NUTCRACKER
ORNAMENT
POINSETTIA
PRESENT
SLEIGH
SNOWFLAKE
STAR
STOCKING
WREATH

Circular Symbol

During the four weeks of Advent, some families light an Advent wreath each evening. The wreath is a symbol of this holy season. On this page, you will find three words that describe the wreath. Unscramble the letters under each word to find out its symbolism.

Holy Time

Lighting the candles of the Advent wreath helps families to keep in mind the holy and religious meaning of Christmas. Can you find the one and only time in the wreath that the word **HOLY** is spelled correctly? Look from left to right, top to bottom, and even diagonally!

CANDLES
symbolize

O E P H

EVERGREEN
symbolizes

EWN EILF

CIRCLE
symbolizes

YNTEERIT

O Y H O L H L Y
L H O H O L L O
H O L L O H O L
O O Y O H O O L L Y H O Y O Y O H L O O
O H L O Y O   L O H L H O
O H O Y H O   H H O L L H
H O L H O   O H L O O
L H O L   O O Y Y
O L L O   H L O Y
L O H L Y   L O H O L
O H O Y L H   H O O O L Y
L O O O L H   H O H H Y L
H Y L O L   H O L L Y
L H L H   Y L H H
O Y Y L H O H O Y L H O Y L Y O
H O L H O L L H O Y L H

O H H O Y O
H O L H O L

Let's color!
Three of the candles are purple, and one candle is pink. The wreath itself is made from green Christmas tree branches.

Angel Voices

Many people believe that after Jesus was born, angels filled the sky with an important message for the world. To find out what the angels had to say, drop the letters into their proper places in the sky. The letters in each column fit in the spaces directly underneath that column, but they may be scrambled.

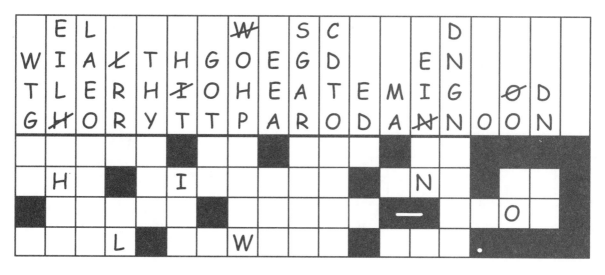

How does one angel greet another angel?

To find the answer to this riddle, you must figure out which way to read around the halo!

Holy Place

Some people visit this place every week. Others go less often, but most visit on Christmas Eve or Christmas Day. Color in the boxes marked with a dot in the upper right-hand corner to find out what this special place is.

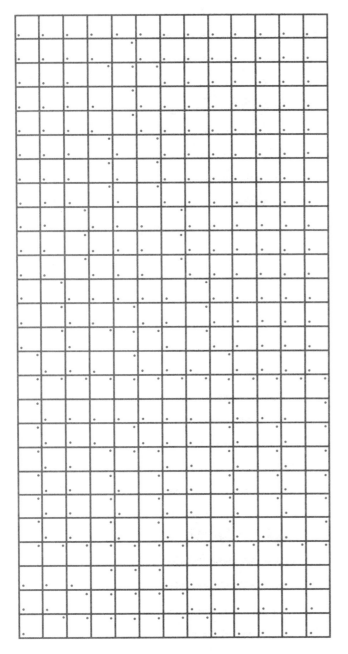

Joyful Noise

Write the letter of each note at the bottom of the page. Then read from left to right to get the name of the most common hymn sung at the end of the Christmas service.

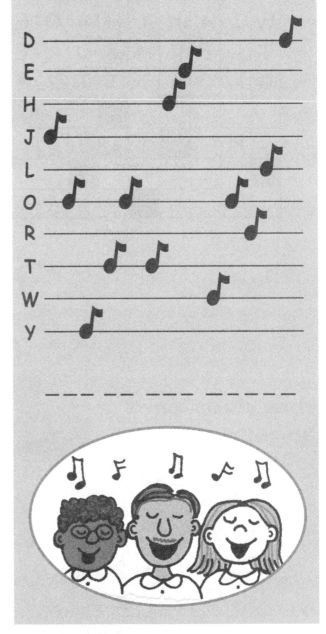

D
E
H
J
L
O
R
T
W
Y

— — — — — — — — — — — — —

Chapter 6

North Pole

Reindeer Games

Unscramble the letters on each line to spell the name of one of Santa's reindeers. When you're finished, read the circled letters from top to bottom to spell out the most famous reindeer of all!

EXTRA FUN: Can you name the one reindeer who is missing from this puzzle?

EADNCR = _ _ _ _ _ _ ◯

PUICD = _ ◯ _ _ _

RENNOD = ◯ _ _ _ _ _

EOCMT = _ ◯ _ _ _

ETIBNZL = _ _ ◯ _ _ _ _

ERNRPAC = ◯ _ _ _ _ _ _

RHADSE = _ _ _ ◯ _ _

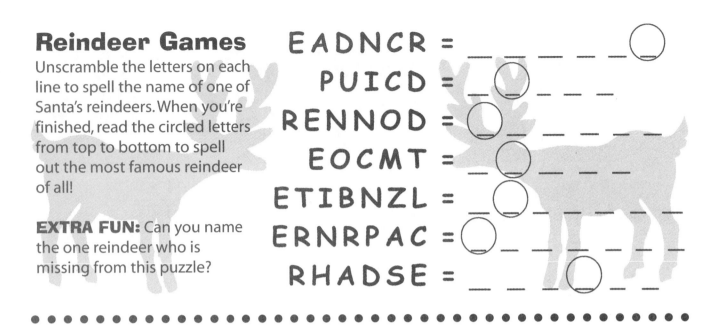

• •

Cool Cash

Do you know where Santa Claus keeps his money? To find out, answer the clues below and fit the letters into their proper place in the grid.

A. Opposite of yes

$$\frac{N}{2} \frac{O}{6}$$

B. To forbid something

$$\overline{8} \ \overline{3} \ \overline{5}$$

C. Opposite of lose

$$\overline{7} \ \overline{1} \ \overline{10}$$

D. Make a request

$$\overline{9} \ \overline{4} \ \overline{11}$$

Why do elves count their money on their toes?

So it doesn't slip through their fingers!

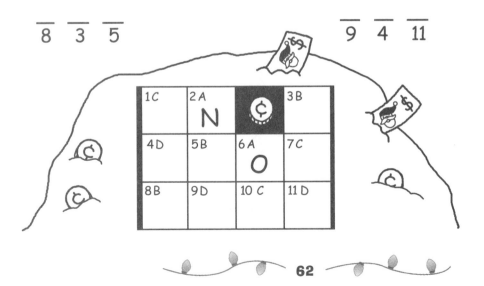

Ho Ho Ho

Can you match the silly answers on the left with the riddles on the right?
Write the correct number on the dotted line.

___ Brrrr-itos!

___ Chimney-changas!

___ Because snow would melt in Africa!

___ A F-rose!

___ North Polish!

___ A flake rake!

___ Rude-olph!

___ The glove compartment!

___ Elf S. Presley!

1. What nationality is Santa Claus?
2. What do you call a reindeer with a red nose and an attitude problem?
3. What kind of flower grows at the North Pole?
4. Which of Santa's elves was a rock'n'roll star?
5. What do the elves order at the North Pole's Mexican restaurant?
6. What does the gardener elf use to keep Santa's yard neat?
7. What does Santa order at the North Pole's Mexican restaurant?
8. Why does it snow at the North Pole?
9. What part of the car keeps your hands warm when driving in the North Pole?

Rolling Riddle

What goes red and white, red and white, red and white?

To find out, read the snowball letters in a spiral, starting with the S in the center.

Crazy Train

Santa has created a super-speedy toy train—the only problem is that none of the elves can catch it to wrap it! Can you get the train to end up in the gift box?

Go See Santa

There are certainly a lot of people waiting to see Santa. Can you spy where each of these small parts is located in the big picture? The parts might be turned sideways or upside-down!

1.
2.
3.
4.
5.
6.

SEE SANTA TODAY

2-6 p.m.

NORTH POLE

Fatten Him Up

First fit all these adjectives into the grid. Then read across the shaded box to discover what kids like about a Santa who is not too skinny!

CHUNKY **PUDGY**
GREAT   **FAT**
STOUT   **BULKY**
HEFTY   **PLUMP**
CHUBBY **WIDE**
LARGE

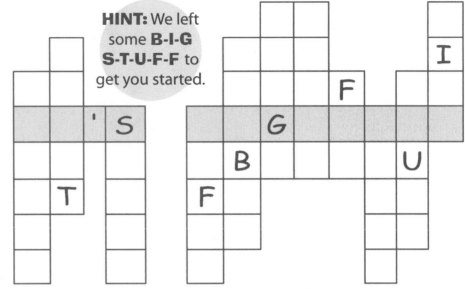

HINT: We left some **B-I-G S-T-U-F-F** to get you started.

Mrs. Claus's Cooking

Building toys is hard work, so Mrs. Claus served a super stew for supper. It was so good that most of the elves asked for more. Can you figure out from the picture how many servings each elf had? How many bowls of stew did Mrs. Claus serve in all?

Sad Santa, Glad Santa

Santa is **SAD** when Christmas is over, but **GLAD** when Christmas comes around again! Cheer up Santa by making a path through the maze, ending with the glad Santa in the bottom right-hand corner. Alternate from **SAD** to **GLAD** by moving up and down, or side to side, but *not* diagonally. If you hit a **SLEEPY** Santa, you are going in the wrong direction!

All Gone!

What two letters of the alphabet describe Santa's sleigh at the end of Christmas day?

To find out, fill in all the triangles in this picture.

Silly Santa

When Santa laughs, he starts a whole lot of words!
See how many of these you can figure out.

H O _ _ = the opening in a chimney

H O _ _ _ = place where travelers pay to sleep

H O _ _ = rubber tube that squirts water

H O _ _ = place where a person lives

H O _ _ = sacred or religious

H O _ _ = keep in a certain position

H O _ _ = story meant to fool people

H O _ _ = wish for something

Santaspeak

Santa has a special language all his own that he only uses when he's at the North Pole. Can you break the code and read the riddle below?

WHOHHOAHOTHO'SHO
YHOEHOLHOLHOOHOWHO
AHONHODHO
GHOOHOEHOSHO
"HHOOHO   HHOOHO
HHOOHO"?
SHOAHONHOTHOAHO
BHOAHONHOAHONHOAHO!

Twin Santas?

These two Santas are almost identical. Can you find the 10 differences between them?

HINT: It doesn't count that they are facing in different directions!

Jingle Yells

Use the clues to fill in the blanks. The last letter of one word is the first letter of the next. **HINT:** It's OK if it looks like you're spelling backward!

1. Middle
2. Pasta packets filled with cheese
3. Round, colored part of the eye
4. One part of a staircase
5. Sandwich bags are made from this
6. Automobile
7. Teacher of the Jewish religion
8. Small hotel, often in a private home
9. To pester constantly
10. Young female
11. Something said that is not true

When you have filled in all the blanks, write the numbered letters on the dotted lines. You will get the answer to this riddle:

What do you call Santa if he goes down a smoking hot chimney by mistake?

"

— — — — —
1 2 3 4 5

— — — — — — **E** "
6 7 8 9 10 11

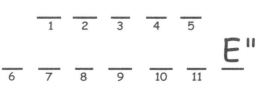

Checking It Twice

Santa is checking his list to see who has been naughty and who has been nice. Find all the words that are similar to "**naughty**" in the left-hand grid, and all the words that are the same as "**nice**" in the other. Why not use two different colored markers to highlight each word as you find it?

AGREEABLE	HONEST	LOYAL	RELIABLE	SPITEFUL
BAD	IMPISH	MEAN	ROUGH	STUBBORN
BULLYING	KIND	MESSY	ROWDY	SWEET
CARING	LOVING	MISCHIEVOUS	RUDE	THOUGHTFUL
DECEITFUL		NEAT		THOUGHTLESS
DISOBEDIENT		OBEDIENT		TRUTHFUL
DISRESPECTFUL		POLITE		UNKIND
FRIENDLY				UNRULY
GENTLE				WELCOMING
HELPFUL				

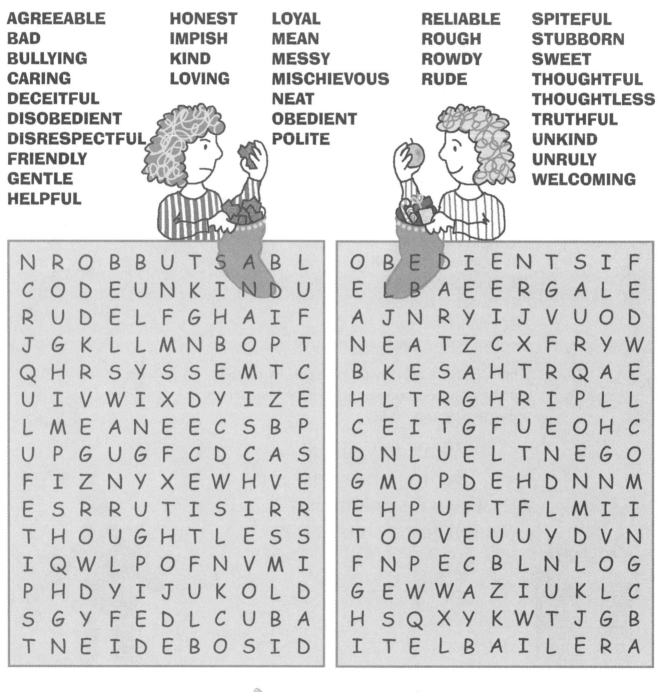

```
N R O B B U T S A B L
C O D E U N K I N D U
R U D E L F G H A I F
J G K L L M N B O P T
Q H R S Y S S E M T C
U I V W I X D Y I Z E
L M E A N E E C S B P
U P G U G F C D C A S
F I Z N Y X E W H V E
E S R R U T I S I R R
T H O U G H T L E S S
I Q W L P O F N V M I
P H D Y I J U K O L D
S G Y F E D L C U B A
T N E I D E B O S I D
```

```
O B E D I E N T S I F
E L B A E E R G A L E
A J N R Y I J V U O D
N E A T Z C X F R Y W
B K E S A H T R Q A E
H L T R G H R I P L L
C E I T G F U E O H C
D N L U E L T N E G O
G M O P D E H D N N M
E H P U F T F L M I I
T O O V E U U Y D V N
F N P E C B L N L O G
G E W W A Z I U K L C
H S Q X Y K W T J G B
I T E L B A I L E R A
```

Letter to Santa

Someone has typed a letter to Santa, but had his or her fingers on the wrong keys! Can you crack this keyboard code so Santa can read his mail?

E3Q4 WQH5Q,

8 YQF3 G33H F346 T99E 5Y8W 63Q4.

0O3QW3 G48HT J3 Q 0Q8H5 W35,

Q 5303WD903, QHE Q 43QOO6 T99E

G99I. 5YQHI 697 F346 J7DY.

6974 R483HE, JQ48WWQ

0.W. YQF3 Q WQR3 5480!

Scrambled Sleigh

Oh no! The elf who was packing Santa's sleigh bumbled the boxes, and some of the letters have fallen off! Unscramble the letters on each box, and add a missing letter from the pile on the ground to make the name of a gift.

What's the difference between the North Pole and the South Pole?

All the difference in the world!

1. _____

2. _____

3. _____

4. _____

5. _____

6. _____

7. _____

8. _____

9. _____

10. _____

11. _____

Oops!

Chapter 7

Sharing Christmas

Holiday Hink Pinks

Even if you don't celebrate Christmas as a religious holiday, you know it is a very hectic time of year. Hink Pinks are perfect for busy people—the answers are a pair of one-syllable words that rhyme. Easy!

What do you call...

...an evergreen that costs nothing?

— — — —

— — — —

...a really nice ringing decoration?

— — — — —

— — — —

...a really fast Santa?

— — — — —

— — — — .

...moving slowly through a crowded shopping center?

— — — —

— — — —

...a not-short Christmas carol?

— — — —

— — — —

What a Pal!

It's fun to visit friends, or "pals," at Christmas. Can you figure out these other words, which all start with the letters **P-A-L**? Choose from the word list, but be careful—there are extra words!

P A L __ __ __
fancy home for a king

P A L __
not bright in color

P A L __ __ __ __
a board on which artists mix colors

P A L __ __ __ __ __
a golden-colored horse

P A L __
inside surface of the hand

P A L __ __ __
mattress made of straw

P A L __ __ __ __ __ __ __
word that is the same backwards or forwards

PALACE	PALFREY
PALATE	PALINDROME
PALAMINO	PALLET
PALATABLE	PALETTE
PALE	PALM
PALISADES	PALPABLE
PALEONTOLOGY	PALTRY

Box It Up

Drew has several presents to mail. Which of these flat cardboard pieces can he fold into perfect gift boxes? Remember, they need to have a top, bottom, and four sides.

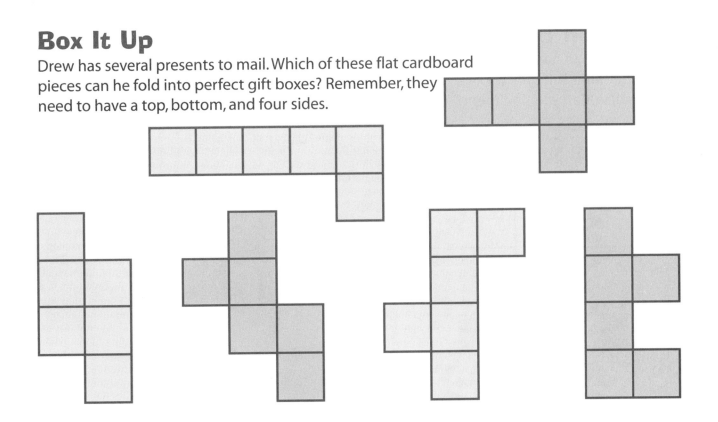

- -

Waiting Game

Now that he's got his boxes, Drew goes to mail his packages. As he enters the post office, Drew meets Dan, Chris, and Charlie. Use the following clues to figure out in what order the boys are standing in line.

1. **Drew is between Charlie and Chris.**

2. **Dan is next to Charlie.**

3. **Chris is not first.**

Stuck on Stamps

These Christmas stamps all look pretty much the same, but only two are exactly alike. Can you find them?

Christmas Letter

Mrs. Walsh was in a hurry when she typed up her holiday letter. She made the same mistake all the way through it. Figure out what she did wrong, and you'll be able to read all the news Mrs. Walsh is sharing with her relatives.

RDECEMBE 3200

RDEA SFRIEND,

EW EHAV NBEE YVER YBUS STHI RYEA!

BBO TGO A WNE BJO DAN EW DMOVE OT WNE YJERSE.

YMAR EWROT A WNE KBOO HWHIC SI GSELLIN LWEL.

MTO SI GLEARNIN OT YPLA ETH TTRUMPE, DAN HSARA DJOINE ETH LGIR SSCOUT.

EW TWEN OT AFLORID NO NVACATIO DAN DHA A DGOO ETIM.

EW EAR LAL LWEL. EHOP UYO EAR, OTO!

ELOV,

BBO, YMAR, MTO, DAN HSARA

76

Address Unknown

These pages have fallen out of your address book. Can you number them in the correct order so they will fit back in alphabetically? **EXTRA FUN:** Figure out what each of the silly names stands for!

Address

Dan D. Lyon

Chris Mass

Clara Nett

Address

Leo Tarred

Bess Twishes

Ed Venture

Address

Bill Ding

Ben Dover

Mary Gold

Knock-knock
> **Who's there?**
Murray.
> **Murray, who?**
Murray Christmas!

Address

Alf Abet

Ted E. Baer

Bar B. Cue

Address

Dee Sember

Moe Skeeto

Chi Spurger

Address

Joe King

Bill Lowney

Hal E. Luya

All Around Town

The Smith family has been looking forward to their Christmas vacation, and they have a big day planned. You must help them get to each place in order. Watch out for one-way streets!

1. Start at **ST. LEO'S** Church to pack holiday food baskets.
2. Travel to the **SENIOR CENTER** to sing Christmas carols.
3. Hurry to the **TRAIN STATION** to pick up Aunt Beth.
4. Meet the Jones's at the **SCIENCE MUSEUM.**

Here We Go A-Caroling

Some friends have decided to share Christmas carols with the neighborhood. Do you know the words to their holiday tunes? Use the four missing letters to fill in the blanks and complete each verse. **HINT:** Letters can be used more than once.

DECK THE HALLS

Missing Letters = D, L, O, T

__ ECK __ HE HA __ __ S WI __ H

B __ UGHS __ F H __ __ __ Y, FA,

__ A, __ A, __ A, __ A, __ A,

__ A, __ A, __ A.

AWAY IN A MANGER

Missing Letters = A, B, S, T

__ W __ Y IN __ M __ NGER,

NO CRI __ FOR __ __ ED.

__ HE LI __ __ LE LORD

JE __ U __ L __ ID DOWN

HI __ __ WEE __ HE __ D.

JINGLE BELLS

Missing Letters: B, N, H, S

JI __ GLE __ ELL __, JI __ GLE __ ELL __,

JI __ GLE ALL T __ E WAY. O __,

W __ AT FU __ IT I __ TO RIDE I __

A O __ E __ OR __ E, OPE __ __ LEIG __.

O COME ALL YE FAITHFUL

Missing Letters = E, C, F, H

O __ OM __ ALL Y __ __ AIT __ __ UL,

JOY __ UL AND TRIUMP __ ANT.

O __ OM __ Y __, O __ OM __

Y __, TO B __ T __ L __ __ __ M.

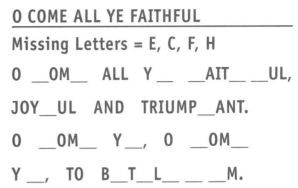

Crazy Caroler

How many different geometric shapes make up this crazy caroler? How many of each kind can you find? Write your answers in the space below.

Family Photos

Many people like to send family pictures at Christmas to relatives they don't get to see very often. Can you tell, just by looking at family resemblances, which one photo went to each of these proud Aunties?

 1.

 2.

 3.

 4.

The More, the Merrier

Christmas is a time when people are happy to share. How many words can you make out of the word **G-E-N-E-R-O-S-I-T-Y**? See if you can make 40! **EXTRA FUN:** Give yourself a pat on the back for every word of five letters or more.

GENEROSITY

1. _____
2. _____
3. _____
4. _____
5. _____
6. _____
7. _____
8. _____
9. _____
10. _____
11. _____
12. _____
13. _____
14. _____
15. _____
16. _____
17. _____
18. _____
19. _____
20. _____

21. _____
22. _____
23. _____
24. _____
25. _____
26. _____
27. _____
28. _____
29. _____
30. _____
31. _____
32. _____
33. _____
34. _____
35. _____
36. _____
37. _____
38. _____
39. _____
40. _____

'Tis the Season

Unscramble each of the words. To find out what Christmas is *really* the season for, write the circled letters, in order, on the line at the bottom. **EXTRA FUN:** Can you see the connection between all the words chosen?

UGH
_ _ (_)

IMSEL
_ _ (_) _ _

VELO
_ _ (_) _

MITE
_ (_) _ _

NEYOM
_ _ _ (_) _ _

TIFG
(_) _ _ _

People Helping People

There are many words to describe qualities of people who give to others without expecting to get anything in return. Work out these word equations and you will discover some of them.

Small wagon - T + Jewelry on a finger = _____

Opposite of bad + Opposite of won't = _____

First half of charcoal + Second half of purity = _____

First half of helpless + Opposite of empty – L = _____

Instrument that points north + Roaring animal – L = _____

First half of symbol + Small trail + Y = _____

• •

Christmas Baskets

Many items have been collected to fill holiday baskets for families in need. But somehow, the digits in the total of each item got mixed up! See if you can rearrange the digits to make the *largest* possible number. Put the correct number in the space provided.

Mittens	226	
Toothbrushes	1734	
Teddy Bears	19	
Hats	154	
Canned Food	4257	
Frozen Turkeys	428	

Knock-knock.

> **Who's there?**

Cargo.

> **Cargo who?**

Cargo, "Vroom, vroom," and deliver all the Christmas baskets!

Secret Santas

Each of these students is a Secret Santa to someone else in the classroom. Look at the present hidden in each gift bag. Match up the student givers and receivers, and fill in the grid below.

	Gives To	Receives From
Tonya		
Ethan		
Matt		
Miguel		
Kate		
Krystal		

Toys for Tots

For almost 50 years, a branch of the United States armed forces has collected toys to give to needy children at Christmas. People buy new, unwrapped toys and leave them in collection boxes at local businesses. Use the coin code to see who is responsible for this wonderful program.

Code: A=1 cent, B=2 cents, C=3 cents, etc.

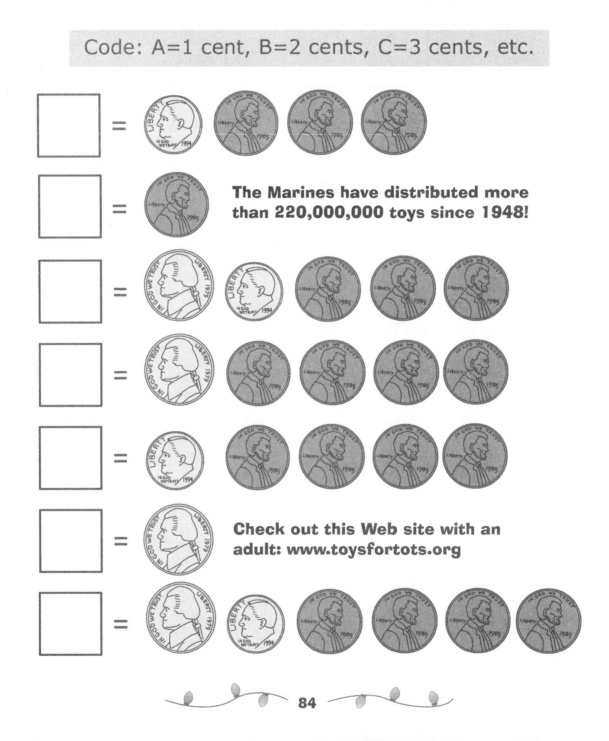

The Marines have distributed more than 220,000,000 toys since 1948!

Check out this Web site with an adult: www.toysfortots.org

Chapter 8

You're Invited

Party Date

Holly is planning to have a Christmas party. Use the clues below to figure out which date she chose. **HINT:** It is helpful to cross out each date that you think Holly did *not* choose.

- It is not on a Saturday.
- It is on a day with a two-digit number.
- It is not on a day that starts with the number 1.
- The two numbers in the date add up to the number 3.

Sun.	Mon.	Tues.	Wed.	Thur.	Fri.	Sat.
❄ ❄ DECEMBER ❄ ❄						
					1	2
3	4	5	6	7	8	9
10	11	12	13	14	15	16
17	18	19	20	21	22	23
24	25	26	27	28	29	30
31						

Luke's List

Luke is planning a Christmas party, too. But something is wrong with his shopping list! Cross out the items that seem to be for totally different kinds of parties. **EXTRA FUN:** What other holidays did Luke have on his mind when he was writing this list?

corn-on-the-cob
candy corn
popcorn balls
iced tea
ice skates
ice cream cones

American flag
"Santa Stops Here" flag
pumpkin
tombstone
tree stand
cider
lemonade
sparklers
colored lights
flashlights
hot chocolate
chocolate bunny
candy canes
jelly beans
scary mask

white beard
rotten eggs
eggnog
plastic eggs
firewood
firecrackers
marshmallows
marshmallow chicks
hotdogs
turkey
tinsel
cobwebs
stockings
baskets
red / blue balloons
red / green balloons

By the Numbers

Jenny wants her tree to look perfect for the big Christmas party. She has carefully figured out where each kind of ornament should go. Complete the equations, and match each answer to a decoration. Draw the ornaments in place to decorate the tree!

EXTRA FUN: Color the page when you are done.

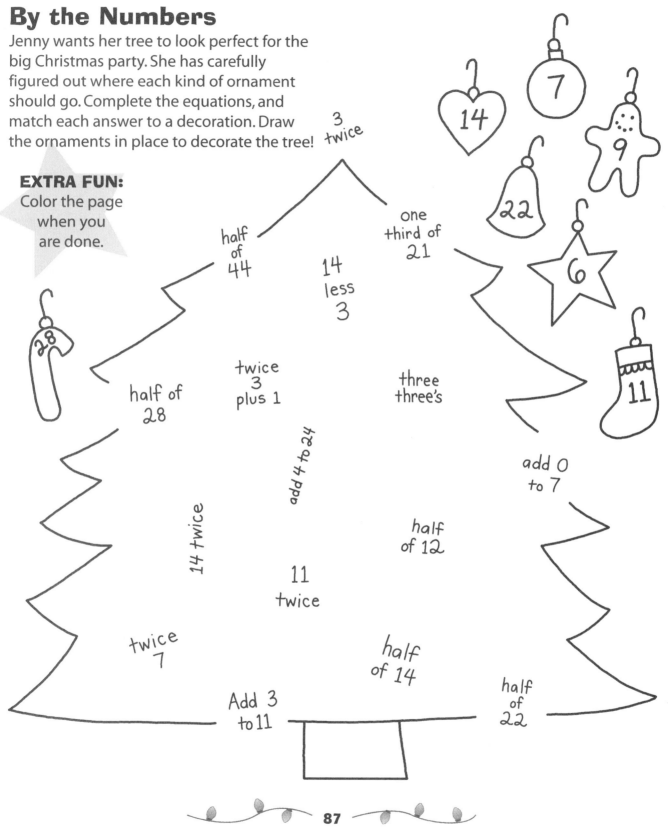

3 twice

one third of 21

half of 44

14 less 3

twice 3 plus 1

three three's

half of 28

add 4 to 24

14 twice

half of 12

add 0 to 7

11 twice

twice 7

half of 14

half of 22

Add 3 to 11

Party Prep

So much to do, so little time. Group together all the words that have the same number in their box. Form a sentence with these words and write it in the blank provided. When you are done, you will have a list of things to do to get ready for your Christmas party.

1. _____

2. _____

3. _____

4. _____

5. _____

6. _____

1 DATE	2 AND	3 SUPPLIES	4 GET	5 THE	6 PARTY
6 AND	1 SET	2 GUESTS	3 LIST	4 PARTY	5 VERY
3 SHOPPING	5 CLEAN	4 FAVORS	1 ON	2 SEND	3 MAKE
5 WELL	3 FOR	6 THE	2 CHOOSE	6 DECORATE	1 YOUR
2 YOUR	4 THE	1 CALENDAR	5 WHOLE	3 A	6 SET
4 GROCERIES	6 TABLE	5 HOUSE	4 AND	2 INVITES	1 A

Fractional Feast

Maxine plans to fill her plate at the buffet. Look at the fractions around the table. They tell you how many items Maxine will take from each different tray. Cross out all the food that she will eat. **HINT:** For each fraction, the bottom number is the same as the number of goodies on one of the trays.

Eggnog, Anyone?

This letter grid is full of eggnog, but the word is only spelled correctly once. Can you find it? The letters can go forward, backward—or even diagonally!

```
G G E O G E E G E E
G E G N E G G E G G
E G G N G O G N G E
N G G G E O N E N G
G O N G O N G G E G
G N O E G G N O O N
E G G N O N G G E O
```

Pass the Bubbly

Find your way from top to bottom through the bubbles in this festive glass of sparkling cider!

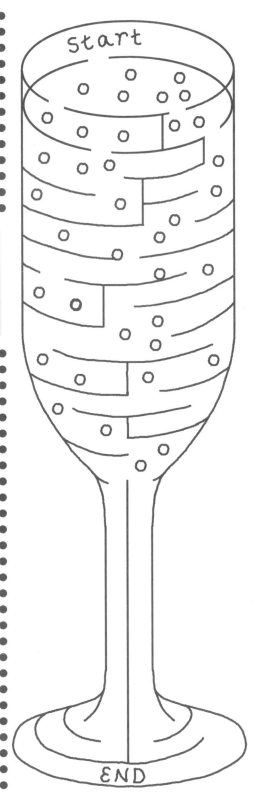

Cookie Filling

Write a letter in the middle space of each column to form a seven-letter word that reads from top to bottom. Then read across the shaded row to answer this riddle:

What do you call someone just learning how to bake small, flat, sweet cakes?

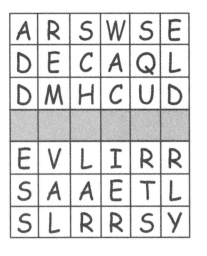

C	R	A	M	I	J
O	E	C	I	N	E
N	C	R	L	S	W
E	V	B	I	S	L
R	E	A	N	T	R
N	R	T	G	S	Y

A	R	S	W	S	E
D	E	C	A	Q	L
D	M	H	C	U	D
E	V	L	I	R	R
S	A	A	E	T	L
S	L	R	R	S	Y

FROS   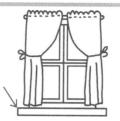 THE

 L

T

Sing-Along

It's fun to figure out which songs to sing at a holiday party. Take a careful look at the pictures and letters on this page. Can you put the bits and pieces together and come up with the titles of eight popular Christmas carols? **HINT:** Some of the items can be used more than once!

1. _____
2. _____
3. _____
4. _____
5. _____
6. _____
7. _____
8. _____

Ⓛ L

O

JING   VER

SHHH!

Pin the ___ on the ___?

"Pin the Tail on the Donkey" is a great game, but not quite right for a Christmas party. Can you create some holiday "Pin the ___ on the ___" alternatives? Choose from the word list.

1. Pin the _____ on the _____.

2. Pin the _____ on the _____.

3. Pin the _____ on the _____.

4. Pin the _____ on the _____.

5. Pin the _____ on the _____.

6. Pin the _____ on the _____.

TREE WREATH BEARD

ANTLERS PRESENT

EARS

BOW REINDEER STAR

DOOR SANTA ELF

Thanks for Inviting Me

It always shows good manners to bring a small present for the person who is hosting a Christmas party. Each of the items in this crossword would make a great "thank you" gift. Can you think of other gifts?

ACROSS
1. Something to play with
5. A candy made from cocoa beans
7. A stick of wax with a wick

DOWN
2. Decoration to hang on the Christmas tree
3. Small, flat, sweet cakes
4. Sheets of paper bound between two covers
6. A poinsettia is a type of _____.

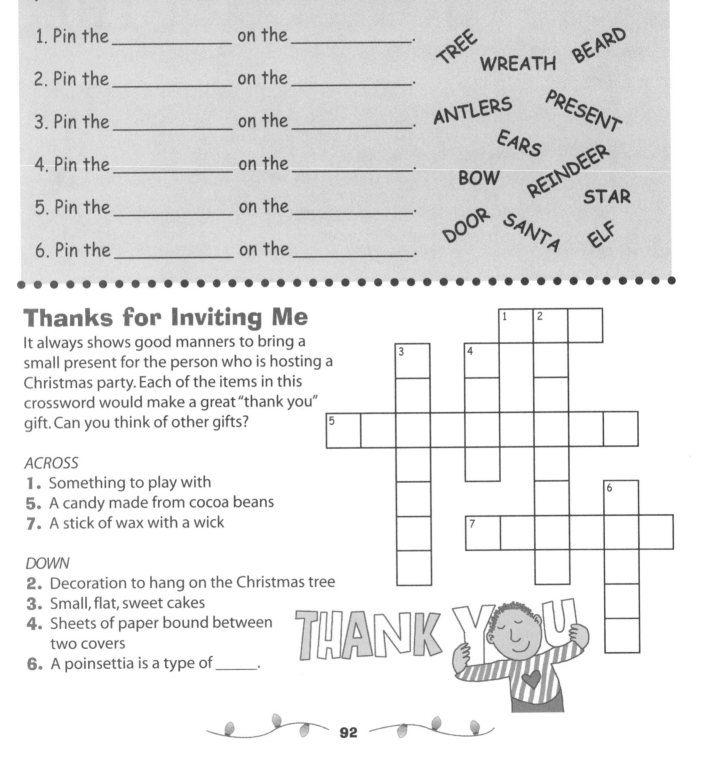

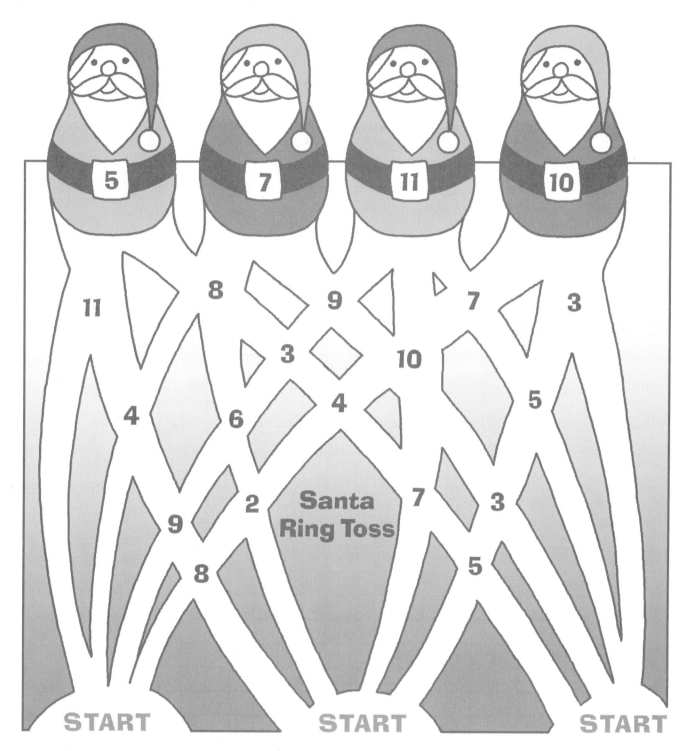

Stand at any of the three starting points to toss your ring. Which path will get you the most points? **HINT:** Don't forget to count the number inside Santa's belt buckle, too!

Grab Bag

What's in the grab bag? Find out by shading in the numbered boxes that are listed for each row (remember, rows go across). Be sure to fill in each box carefully from left to right. **SPECIAL DIRECTIONS:** If there is a set of numbers with a dash between them (for example, 5-16), that means you must shade in box 5, box 16, and *all* the numbers in between!

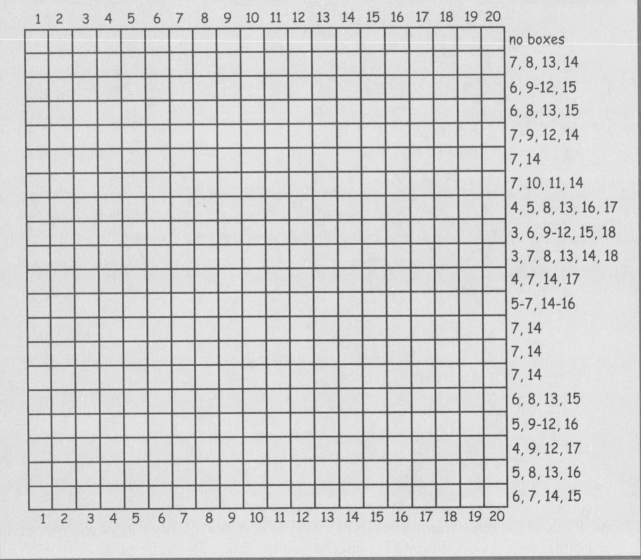

no boxes
7, 8, 13, 14
6, 9-12, 15
6, 8, 13, 15
7, 9, 12, 14
7, 14
7, 10, 11, 14
4, 5, 8, 13, 16, 17
3, 6, 9-12, 15, 18
3, 7, 8, 13, 14, 18
4, 7, 14, 17
5-7, 14-16
7, 14
7, 14
7, 14
6, 8, 13, 15
5, 9-12, 16
4, 9, 12, 17
5, 8, 13, 16
6, 7, 14, 15

Where's the Party?

You'll find the party if you cross out all of the following kinds of words on the paths to each door. Then read the words that are left over!

- Words with **PP** in them
- Words that rhyme with **CLOCK**
- Words that start with **PR**
- Words that end with **D**

When you find the right house, add up the numbers along that pathway to see what time the party starts.

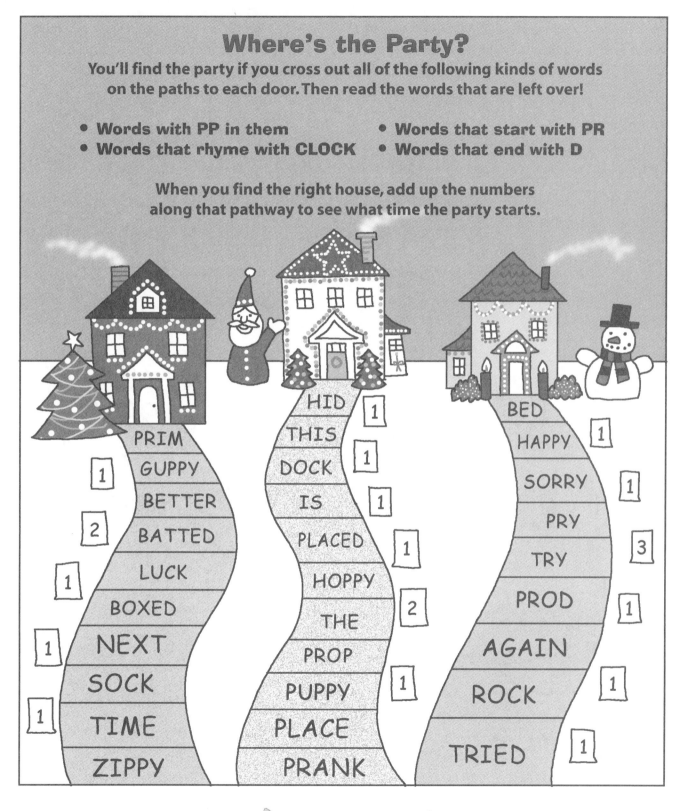

Path 1 (left): PRIM · GUPPY · BETTER · BATTED · LUCK · BOXED · NEXT · SOCK · TIME · ZIPPY
Numbers: 1, 2, 1, 1, 1

Path 2 (middle): HID · THIS · DOCK · IS · PLACED · HOPPY · THE · PROP · PUPPY · PLACE · PRANK
Numbers: 1, 1, 1, 1, 2, 1

Path 3 (right): BED · HAPPY · SORRY · PRY · TRY · PROD · AGAIN · ROCK · TRIED
Numbers: 1, 1, 3, 1, 1, 1

And to All, a Good Night

What is an excellent way to relax after your Christmas party? Connect the dots to find out!
EXTRA FUN: Find the two dots without numbers. Draw a pom-pom around each one.

really nice, really good, really magical

Christmas!

Chapter 9

Christmas Stories

Christmas Characters

Many of our favorite holiday stories have been captured on film. Watching them over and over, year after year, they become part of our Christmas traditions. Do you recognize any of the characters in this crossword puzzle?

ACROSS

2. Girl who didn't believe in Santa
3. Girl who gets a nutcracker
5. Jolly fellow dressed in red and white
8. The Grinch's dog
12. He tried to stop Christmas
14. Snoopy's owner
16. Charlie Brown's dog
17. The "other" reindeer
18. Elf who wants to be a dentist

DOWN

1. _____ Cornelius was looking for gold at the North Pole
4. The_____ Snowman was a North Pole beast
5. The_____ _____ fairy led the waltz of the flowers
6. Real name of department store Santa
7. Tiny Tim's father,_____ Cratchitt
9. Snowman who comes to life
10. Stingy man visited by three ghosts
11. Small, sickly boy
12. Mother _____ had puppets hidden under her huge skirt
13. The youngest Who in Whoville
15. Reindeer with the red nose

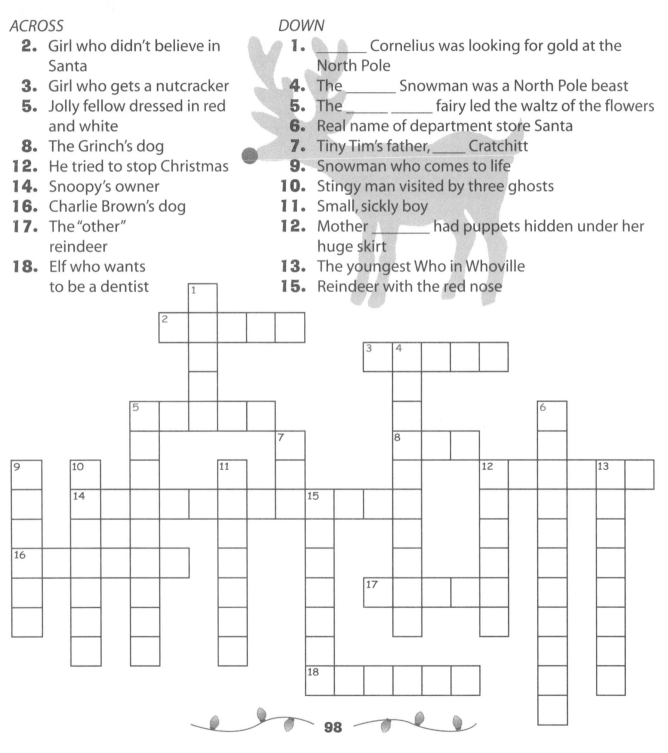

Story Starter

Do you know what the story *A Night Before Christmas* was originally titled? Cross out the following words, then read the remaining words from left to right and top to bottom:

Cross out all the words that rhyme with **D-E-E-R**
Cross out all the words that start with the letter **C**
Cross out all the two-letter words with an **O**
Cross out all the words that rhyme with **P-O-P**
Cross out all the words that end in **E-D**
Cross out all the words that start with **S-L**

SO	A	SLEIGH	ON	TOP
CANDY	DROP	OR	VISIT	BED
CHOP	SLOW	CAROL	RED	HEAR
FED	GO	FROM	TO	CHIMNEY
CHRIST	HOP	NEAR	SLIP	CARDS
NO	SAINT	PEER	STOP	HEED
CHURCH	LED	NICHOLAS	YEAR	REAR

· ·

Dancing Story

Put a letter in the middle space to form a three-letter word that reads from top to bottom. When you're finished, read the shaded boxes from left to right. If you have chosen the correct words, you will learn the name of a famous ballet that is based on a popular Christmas story.

O	F	A	I	T	P	A	S	R	C
	U			A		K			
E	N	E	E	Y	T	E	I	D	Y

Perfect Present

Imagine that you have picked out the perfect book as a present for a special friend. Use colored pencils or crayons to decorate this book plate. Be sure to write a special message!

This book belongs to:

With love from:

Christmas Classic

This book has been in the library so long that the letters have partly worn off. Can you figure out the title and author? **HINT:** The story features the ghosts of Christmas Past, Present, and Future!

A CHRISTMAS CAROL
BY CHARLES DICKENS

Bulging Bookcase

John *had* a whole bookshelf full of holiday books, but his cat knocked them all off! Can you reshelf the books into the blank spaces? Make sure to write the titles in alphabetical order.

EXTRA FUN: Get the mouse through the maze of books and back to his hole before the cat wakes up!

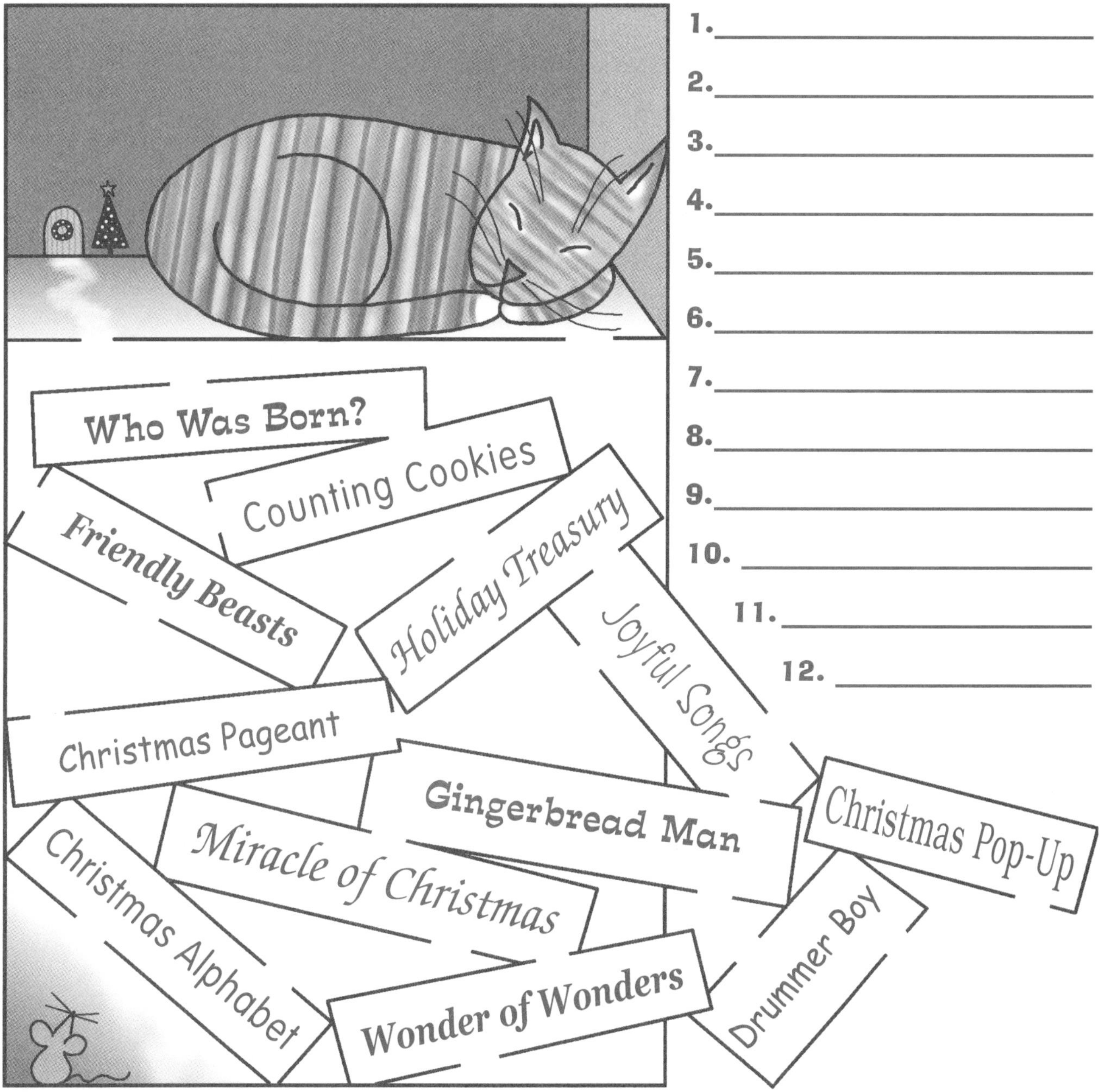

1. _____

2. _____

3. _____

4. _____

5. _____

6. _____

7. _____

8. _____

9. _____

10. _____

11. _____

12. _____

Who Was Born?

Counting Cookies

Friendly Beasts

Holiday Treasury

Joyful Songs

Christmas Pageant

Gingerbread Man

Christmas Pop-Up

Miracle of Christmas

Christmas Alphabet

Wonder of Wonders

Drummer Boy

The Christmas Crazies

Ask a friend or someone in your family to help create this silly Christmas story. Don't show them the story first! Just ask them for the kind of word you need for each blank spot (the description is written underneath each blank line). Write the words your helper gives you in the blanks, then read the story out loud. It will surely make you laugh! **HINT:** Use a pencil so you can do it again with different words.

It was Christmas morning. _____ , _____
                                  name #1   name #2

and _____ came _____ down the
         name #3   verb ending in "ing"

stairs. They started _____ their gifts.
                        a different verb ending in "ing"

"_____ !" said _____ . "I got a
      exclamation   name #1

_____ _____ ." "_____!" said
    color   thing #1   a different exclamation

_____ . "I love this _____ _____ ."
   name #2   adjective   thing #2

"_____ !" said _____ . "I've always
   a different exclamation   name #3

wanted a _____ ." Just then, Mom and Dad came
              thing #3

_____ into the room.
a different verb ending in "ing"

    "Merry _____ !" they said. "Time for
              name of a holiday

_____ . Anybody want some _____?"
      a meal   kind of food

"Merry _____ to you, too!" said
          name of another holiday

_____ and _____ . "Let's eat!"
     name #1   name #2

    "_____ !" yelled _____ ,
      a different exclamation   name #3

" Then we can all _____ together!"
                        activity

102

Scary Christmas?

Christmas stories often feature cheerful elves or beautiful angels. But the story of *The Nutcracker* features a fierce villain! To find out his name, answer the questions below. Write the answers on the dotted lines, then transfer the letters into the numbered boxes in the grid.

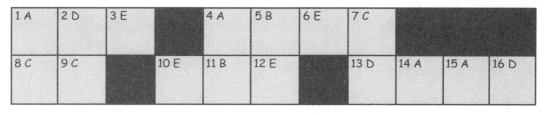

1 A	2 D	3 E		4 A	5 B	6 E	7 C		
8 C	9 C		10 E	11 B	12 E		13 D	14 A	15 A	16 D

A. Sound a clock makes

— — — —
1 14 15 4

B. Short form of hello

— —
11 5

C. Cloud close to the ground

— — —
9 8 7

D. Border of a piece of cloth

— — —
2 16 13

E. Person aged 13 to 19

— — — —
10 3 12 6

Not Your Average Mouse

In addition to being fierce, the King of the Mice had a strange appearance. Collect the letters as you wind through the maze. Read them in order, and you will learn what made him so unusual.

START

END

Nutty Nutcrackers

Can you find the 12 differences between these two nutcrackers?

EXTRA FUN: Try tracing one of the nutcrackers onto a plain piece of paper. Then color him!

The Little Drummer Boy

This famous Christmas carol tells the story of a poor boy who does not think that he has a proper gift to give to Jesus. All he owns is his drum and he ends up pleasing Jesus by playing it for him. Can you tell which of these drums belongs to the boy? It has all the following characteristics:

★ Thick strap   ★ Three Xs

★ Rounded bottom   ★ Pattern on edge 〰〰〰

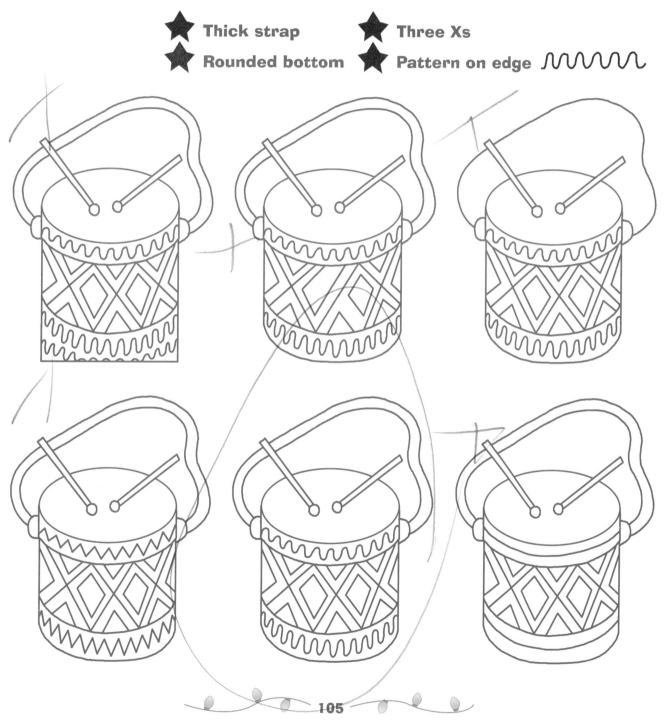

Picture This

Look at the six pictures below. Can you number them correctly so that the story makes sense?

Not a Creature Was Stirring...

Can you find the 10 sleeping creatures (other than Grandpa) hiding in the cozy living room on the next page?

**BEAR
BUNNY
BUTTERFLY
DUCK
FISH
FLAMINGO
HORSE
MOUSE
SNAKE
SEA TURTLE**

What's the difference between a mouse and a house? One letter!

Santa's Goodbye

ΙΛΕΡΚΥ CΙΙRIS⁻ΙΛΛS ⁻O Λ__,

(Finish the letters.)

(Connect the dots.)

(Color "G" squares GREEN, "R" squares RED, and leave "O" squares uncolored.)

O	O	O	O	O	G	O	O	G	O	O	G	O	G	G	O	O	O	O	O	R	R	R	O	R	R	R	O	O	O	O
O	O	O	O	G	O	G	O	G	G	O	G	O	G	O	G	O	O	O	O	O	R	O	O	R	O	R	O	O	O	O
O	O	O	O	G	G	G	O	G	O	G	G	O	G	O	G	O	O	O	O	O	R	O	O	R	O	R	O	O	O	O
O	O	O	O	G	O	G	O	G	O	O	G	O	G	G	O	O	O	O	O	R	O	O	R	R	R	O	O	O	O	O
O	O	O	O	O	O	O	O	O	O	O	O	O	O	O	O	O	O	O	O	O	O	O	O	O	O	O	O	O	O	O
O	G	O	O	G	O	O	G	O	O	O	O	R	O	O	O	O	G	G	O	G	G	O	O	G	G	G	O	G	G	O
G	O	G	O	O	G	O	O	O	R	O	R	O	O	G	O	O	O	G	G	O	G	O	G	O	G	O	G	O	G	G
G	G	G	O	G	O	O	O	G	O	O	R	R	R	O	O	G	O	G	O	G	O	G	O	G	O	G	O	G	O	G
G	O	G	O	G	G	O	O	O	R	O	R	O	O	G	G	O	G	G	G	O	G	G	G	O	G	G	G	O	G	O
O	O	O	O	O	O	O	O	O	O	O	O	O	O	O	O	O	O	O	O	O	O	O	O	O	O	O	O	O	O	O
O	O	O	O	O	O	R	O	O	R	O	R	O	O	R	R	O	O	O	R	O	R	O	R	R	R	O	O	O	O	O
O	O	O	O	O	O	R	R	O	R	O	R	O	R	O	R	O	O	R	O	R	O	R	O	O	R	O	O	O	O	O
O	O	O	O	O	O	R	O	R	R	O	R	O	R	O	R	O	O	R	O	R	O	R	O	O	R	O	O	O	O	O
O	O	O	O	O	O	R	O	R	O	R	O	R	O	R	R	R	O	R	O	R	O	R	O	O	R	O	O	O	O	O

Appendix A

Christmas: The Season of Giving

The true meaning of Christmas is not about what you *get*, but rather about what you *give*. You are never too young to experience the joy that comes from doing nice things for other people without expecting anything in return. Consider doing one or more of the following—not just at Christmas, but all year long!

Donate Toys

★ Clean out your room and find toys that are still in good condition. Donate them to a local homeless shelter.

★ Pick a tag off a "giving tree" and purchase a special toy that a needy child really wants.

★ Buy a new toy and put it in a Toys for Tots box (see page 84 for more about the Toys for Tots program).

Donate Food

★ Many communities prepare food baskets at Christmas—get your friends together and contribute some items!

★ Clip coupons and buy nonperishable items for a local soup kitchen.

★ Take one item from your cart each time you shop and place it in a collection box.

Donate Clothing

★ Many churches welcome clean used clothes that you've outgrown.

★ Buy a new shirt (or jeans, sneakers, etc.) for someone else rather than for yourself.

Donate Books

★ Look through your bookshelf and choose books that you feel you could part with—and other children might enjoy.

★ Buy some of your "favorites" and make them available to schools or shelters.

Donate Money

★ Save a portion of your allowance all year and give the lump sum to your favorite charity.

★ Drop a quarter into the Salvation Army bucket every time you pass one during the holiday season.

Donate Yourself

★ Volunteer to help when any opportunity presents itself.

★ Do random acts of kindness. Call Grandma to say "I love you" ... shovel a neighbor's walkway ... serve Mom breakfast. You will put a smile on someone else's face—and your own, too!

Appendix B

Christmas Wish List

What I would like from Santa:

What I would like Santa to bring my family:

I will leave this snack for Santa:

Puzzle Answers

page v · **Introduction**

```
N P E A C E F U L
T O S Q U I T V H
R G I H U S H E D
A F L S R S W H I
N E E P E C A L M
Q D N X O L E F J
U C T A B N E G K
I B Y Z C D M S L
L A S E R E N E S
```

page 2 · **Ancient Origins**
Possible answers:

ail	natu	runt	star
art	ral	rust	sun
last	rail	rut	tail
lint	rain	sail	tan
list	ran	sat	tar
lit	rant	sin	tin
lunar	rat	sit	turn
lust	ruin	slant	
nail	run	snail	

page 2 · **Pucker Up**

```
I M P
S I T
A S K
I T S
O L D
P E G
A T E
W O N
L E D
```

page 2 · **To Market, to Market**
The English translation for the name of this famous German shopping place is "Christ Child Market."

page 3 · **Christmas Greetings**
ACROSS
1. Vietnam (Chuc Mung Giang Sinh)
4. Brazil (Boas Festas)
7. France (Joyeux Noel)
8. Mexico (Feliz Navidad)
19. Egypt (Mboni Chrismen)

DOWN
2. Sweden (God Jul)
3. Ireland (Nollaig Shona Dhuit)
5. Germany (Frohliche Weihnachten)
9. Yugoslavia (Cestitamo Bozic)
17. Italy (Buon Natale)

The familiar American greeting reads: We wish you a merry Christmas!

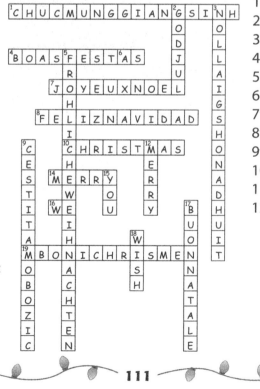

page 4 · **Gift-Giver**

FATHER CHRISTMAS
PERE NOEL
LA BEFANA
KRIS KRINGLE
BABOUSHKA

page 4 · **Nice Neighbor**

CANADA SENDS THOUSANDS OF CHRISTMAS TREES!

page 5 · **The 12 Days of Christmas**
1st day = partridge in a pear tree
2nd day = 2 turtle doves
3rd day = 3 French hens
4th day = 4 calling birds
5th day = 5 golden rings
6th day = 6 geese a-laying
7th day = 7 swans a-swimming
8th day = 8 maids a-milking
9th day = 9 drummers drumming
10th day = 10 pipers piping
11th day = 11 ladies dancing
12th day = 12 lords a-leaping

Puzzle Answers

page 6 • **Hidden Angels**

BOOKSTORE
TOY
BEST SELLERS

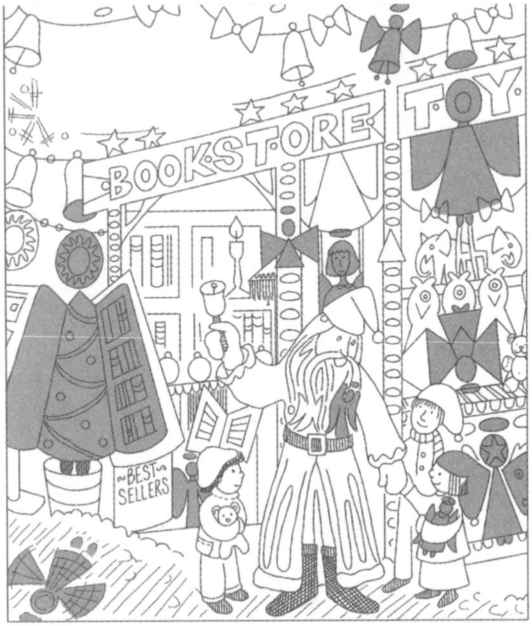

page 8 • **Sweet Sweden**

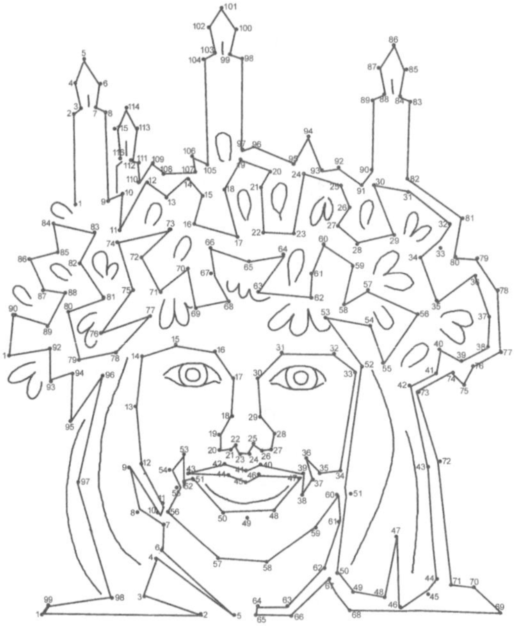

page 7 • **What's Xmas?**

START
XMAS
END

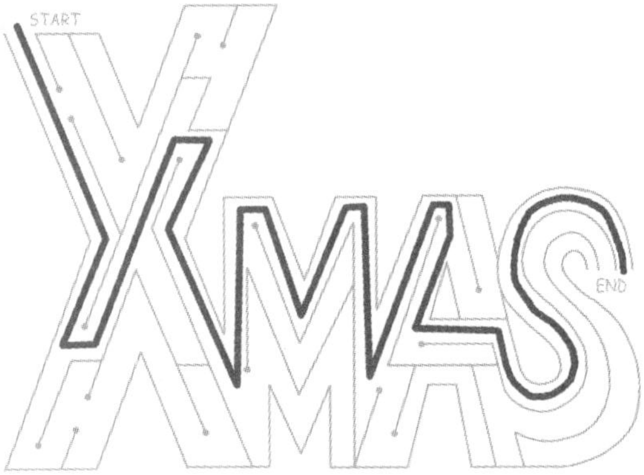

page 7 • **Fill It Up!**

RITHS = SHIRT

AHT = HAT

OTCA = COAT

TIETNMS = MITTENS

NSATP = PANTS

page 9 • **Popular Poppers**

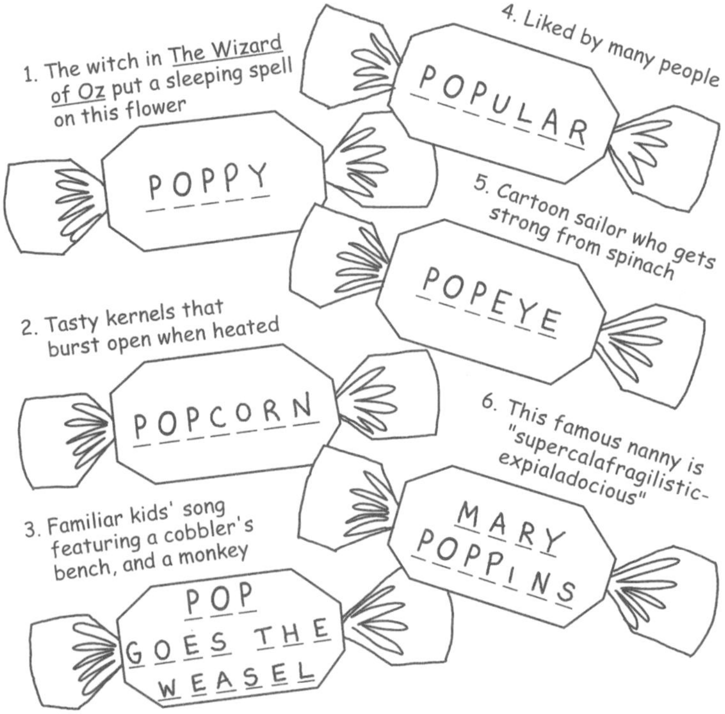

1. The witch in The Wizard of Oz put a sleeping spell on this flower
POPPY
2. Tasty kernels that burst open when heated
POPCORN
3. Familiar kids' song featuring a cobbler's bench, and a monkey
POP GOES THE WEASEL
4. Liked by many people
POPULAR
5. Cartoon sailor who gets strong from spinach
POPEYE
6. This famous nanny is "supercalafragilistic-expialadocious"
MARY POPPINS

Puzzle Answers

page 10 · Greek Greetings

1F T	2J H	3B E	4I Y		5E D	6G E	7A C	8C O	9H R	10G A	11D T	12G E
	13G T	14A H	15K E	16A I	17K R		18E B	19D O	20K A	21K T	22G S	
23D W	24E I	25K T	26C H		27H B	28A L	29E U	30I E		31H A	32H N	33A D
	34B W	35I H	36J I	37B T	38F E		39E L	40B I	41C G	42B H	43F T	44G S

THEY DECORATE THEIR BOATS WITH BLUE AND WHITE LIGHTS

A. A young boy or girl
C H I L D
7 14 16 28 33

B. The color of snow
W H I T E
34 42 40 37 3

C. A fully grown pig
H O G
26 8 41

D. The number after one
T W O
11 23 19

E. Put together piece by piece
B U I L D
18 29 24 39 5

F. Try something new
T E S T
43 38 44 1

G. To annoy playfully
T E A S E
13 6 10 22 12

H. Building where farm animals live
B A R N
27 31 9 32

I. A word used to call someone
H E Y
35 30 4

J. Short way of saying hello
H I
2 36

K. A special sweet snack
T R E A T
21 17 15 20 25

page 12 · Favorite Flower

P	two after N
O	four before S
I	one before J
N	four after J
S	between R and T
E	the fifth one
T	three after Q
T	two before V
I	between H and J
A	the first one

page 11 · Warm Wishes

page 12 · Pretty Parols

Puzzle Answers

page 14 · **Wishful Thinking**

If you read only the capital letters, you will find out that Mom is secretly hoping for a ROCKER, Dad would like a CAMERA, Megan would love to get some MAKEUP, Timmy would be really surprised if he got a GUITAR, Dora would enjoy a RATTLE, and Pepper the dog wants a new COLLAR.

page 15 · **Bow Tie**

The secret is that Kayla ties her *arms* in a knot before she picks up the ribbon. Try it! First, fold your arms over and under as you see in this drawing. Bend to pick up one end of the ribbon with one hand. Then bend the other way to pick up the other end of the ribbon with the other hand. Hold on tight, and as you slowly untie your arms, you will tie the ribbon into a knot. It's like magic!

page 15 · **Who Gets What?**

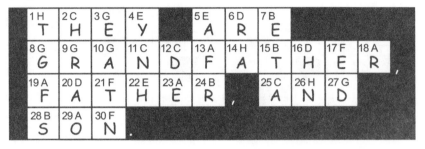

A. To show a desire to do something
$\underset{29}{O}\ \underset{13}{F}\ \underset{19}{F}\ \underset{23}{E}\ \underset{18}{R}$

B. To stop working
$\underset{24}{R}\ \underset{7}{E}\ \underset{28}{S}\ \underset{15}{T}$

C. Your fingers are part of this
$\underset{2}{H}\ \underset{25}{A}\ \underset{11}{N}\ \underset{12}{D}$

D. A cheerleader's cheer
$\underset{6}{R}\ \underset{20}{A}\ \underset{16}{H}$

E. Dried grass for horses
$\underset{22}{H}\ \underset{5}{A}\ \underset{4}{Y}$

F. The number after nine
$\underset{21}{T}\ \underset{17}{E}\ \underset{30}{N}$

G. The year you are in school
$\underset{8}{G}\ \underset{9}{R}\ \underset{10}{A}\ \underset{27}{D}\ \underset{3}{E}$

H. A light brown color
$\underset{1}{T}\ \underset{14}{A}\ \underset{26}{N}$

page 16 · **Squiggle Giggles**

Here is what we think is inside the boxes. Your drawings will probably look different than ours.

Puzzle Answers

page 17 · **Pretty Packages**

page 17 · **Giving Gifts**

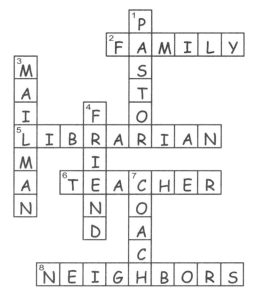

page 18–19 · **Picking the Perfect Present**

Possible choices for Alex:
Soccer ball ($15.00)
Stopwatch ($18.00)
Baseball bat ($8.95)
Hockey stick ($16.75)
Inline skates ($30.00)
Baseball caps ($8.90 each)
Whistle ($1.95)

Possible choices for Jason:
Plastic flamingo ($5.75)
Bird book ($9.95)
Gorilla poster ($4.95)
Goldfish in bowl ($8.75)
Plastic spider ($1.75)
Tiger stuffed animal ($24.95)
Lizard T-shirt ($11.95)

Possible choices for Allison:
"I Love Crafts" smock ($6.15)
Paint set ($6.95)
Brushes ($6.95)
Yarn ($2.95)
Knitting needles ($4.95)
Easel ($25.00)
Glitter ($2.25)

For exactly $20, Brian can buy a baseball cap for Alex ($8.90), the gorilla poster for Jason ($4.95), and the "I Love Crafts" smock for Allison ($6.15)

Puzzle Answers

page 20 · **Missing Package**

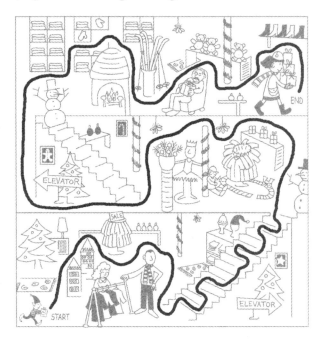

page 22 · **Gift Tags**

Don't worry if your answers don't match up! A few of these allow for different answers. For example, you may have thought of "May" instead of "April."

page 21 · **Presents Hink Pinks**

1. What do you call a present that arrives very quickly?

   S W I F T   G I F T

2. What do you have when you accidentally break two presents?

   D O U B L E   T R O U B L E

3. What do you see when your brother opens the perfect present?

   B O Y   J O Y

4. What do you call the light that shines off the looped ribbon on top of a present?

   B O W   G L O W

5. What do you call it when you cut the wrapping paper the wrong way?

   S N I P   S L I P

6. What do you call a kid who rips open all the presents on Christmas morning?

   W I L D   C H I L D

7. What do you call a nice gift?

   P L E A S A N T

   P R E S E N T

page 21 · **Wacky Word**

Answer: Santa Paws!

F L R S U O
A F N R V
T V E Y R
R A O V U
P F V L A E
U W F F L
R F S Y R O

page 23 · **All Wrapped Up**

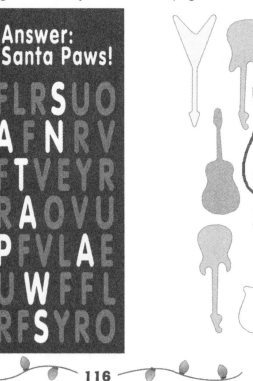

Puzzle Answers

page 24 · Where Are the Presents?

page 27 · Ornament Scramble

1. POPCORN
2. FRUIT
3. CANDY
4. COOKIES
5. CANDLES
6. BELLS

BONUS: PICKLE

page 27 · The Perfect Tree

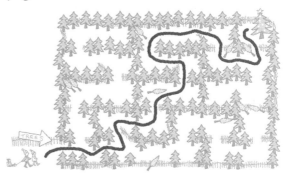

page 26 · Oh, Christmas Tree

Read the letters from left to right, and top to bottom:
"The tradition started in Germany."

page 28 · Which Wreath?
The wreath with the odd number of lights does not belong.

page 28 · Stuff the Stocking

117

Puzzle Answers

page 29 • **String of Lights**

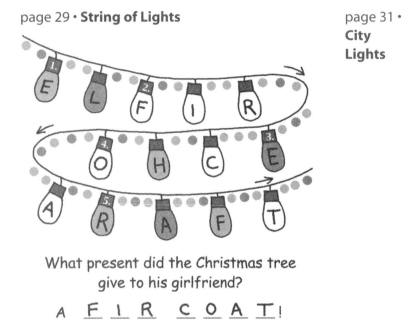

What present did the Christmas tree give to his girlfriend?

A <u>F I R</u> <u>C O A T</u>!

page 30 • **How Symbolic**

page 31 • **City Lights**

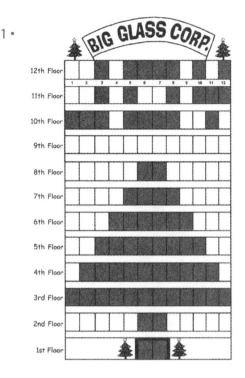

page 32 • **Yard Art**

page 33 • **Christmas Rings**

<u>THE</u> <u>CHRISTMAS</u> ☆
<u>ALPHABET</u> <u>HAS</u> ☆
<u>NO</u> <u>L</u>. <u>GET</u> <u>IT</u>? <u>NOEL</u>!

Puzzle Answers

page 34 • Oops!

page 34 • Candles

N	E	I	R			
A	A	N	D	Y	E	
B	L	R	T	L	S	S
S	H	O	A	H	E	R
C	U	W	N	T	E	R
N	E	I	T	H	E	R
C	A	N	D	L	E	S
A	L	W	A	Y	S	
B	U	R	N			
S	H	O	R	T	E	R	!

page 35 • Red and Green and . . .

Another Christmas color: G O L D

C A N D L E

R U D O L P H ' S N O S E

B O W

S T O C K I N G

M I S T L E T O E

T R E E

Another Christmas color: S I L V E R

I V Y

W R E A T H

page 36 • Evergreen

EVER	GLADE	UP	SET	DOWN
GREEN	LAND	FILL	FAST	FOOD
HOUSE	HOLD	DAY	BREAK	FOR
FLY	UP	SOME	WHAT	EVER
PAPER	RIGHT	HAND	FULL	GREEN

page 36 • Simply Snowflakes

page 38–39 • Getting Groceries

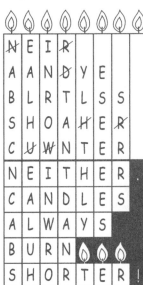

Puzzle Answers

page 38 · Missing Cake
This picture puzzle is an optical illusion—turn the page upside down, and you will see the "missing" piece of cake right in the pan!

page 40 · How Many Marshmallows?
Jeremy (6), John (4), Jennifer (3), Joshua (2), Jessica (3), and Justin (2).

page 40 · Santa Snacks

page 41 · Sweet Riddle

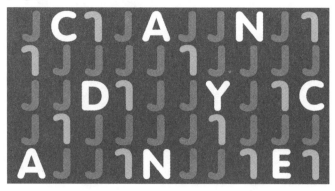

page 41 · Mmm Mmm . . . Good!

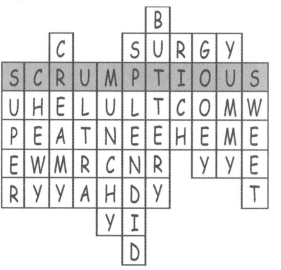

page 42 · Cookie Questions

A. Belongs to me
M Y
16 18

B. Rounded back part of the foot
H E E L
1 7 8 9

C. Enjoyment
F U N
6 15 11

D. Anything against the law
C R I M E
13 14 10 17 2

E. A happy dog does this with his tail
W A G S
3 4 12 5

1B	2D		3E	4E	5E	
H	E		W	A	S	
6C	7B	8B	9B	10D	11C	12E
F	E	E	L	I	N	G
13D	14D	15C	16A	17D	18A	
C	R	U	M	M	Y	!

XJUI DPPLJF
W I T H C O O K I E

TIFFUT
S H E E T S

For each letter in the message, substitute the letter that comes before it in the alphabet.

Puzzle Answers

page 43 · Gingerbread Village

Castle = $25.00
School = $23.00
Ski Chalet = $25.50 (most expensive)
Church = $22.50
Barn = $24.50

page 44 · Look! Good Food

Beth _TOOK_ a _GOOD_ _LOOK_ in the _COOK_ _BOOK_.

"I will bake some _COOK_ies," she said.

"I will start _SOON_ and they will be done by _NOON_. Beth _ZOOM_ed around the kitchen and made some _COOK_ie dough. She opened the oven _DOOR_ and slid a tray in. When the _COOK_ies were done, she _TOOK_ them out to _COOL_. Those _COOK_ies put her family in a really _GOOD_ _MOOD_!

page 45 · Cookie Dough

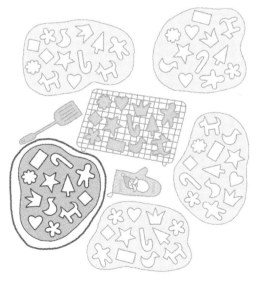

page 46 · Look Alikes / Mixed Mints

page 47 · Tasty Treats

🍬 White and Red Garlands 🍬

popped _CORN_,
raw _CRANBERRIES_,
needle, heavy _THREAD_

🍬 Crunchy Fudge 🍬

CHOCOLATE chips,
chopped _NUTS_, salt,
condensed milk, vanilla

🍬 Fruitcake 🍬

flour, sugar, baking powder,
salt, eggs, vanilla, dates,
candied _CHERRIES_,
dried _APRICOTS_

🍬 Gingerbread Men 🍬

butter, sugar, flour, baking soda,
nutmeg, _GINGER_, salt,
MOLASSES,
COOKIE cutters

🍬 Cheesecake 🍬

GRAHAM cracker crumbs,
sugar, butter, eggs, vanilla,
CREAM CHEESE,
sour _CREAM_

🍬 Apple Pie 🍬

pastry _CRUSTS_, sugar,
flour, green _APPLES_, butter

Puzzle Answers

page 48 · **Santa Sundae**

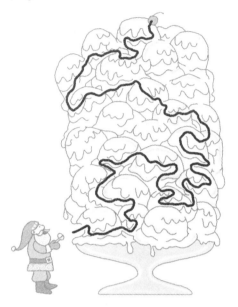

page 51 · **No Room at the Inn**

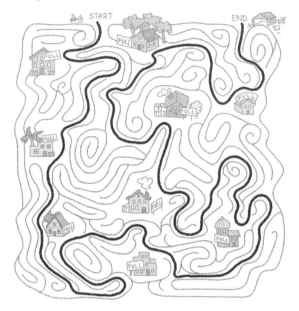

page 50 · **The Story Behind Christmas**

~~BEST~~	CHRISTMAS	~~TREE~~	IS	~~BAKE~~
A	~~AN~~	HOLIDAY	~~TRUST~~	INTENDED
~~TRY~~	~~TROUBLE~~	~~AX~~	~~BATH~~	~~TRUMPET~~
~~AS~~	TO	~~TRAP~~	CELEBRATE	~~AT~~
THE	~~TRAVEL~~	BIRTH	~~EAR~~	OF
~~TREASURE~~	JESUS	~~JAR~~	CHRIST	~~CAR~~

Answer: Christmas is a holiday intended to
celebrate the birth of Jesus Christ.

page 50 · **For Goodness' Sake**

1. Wonder
2. Friendship
3. Calm
4. Love
5. Peace

page 52 · **Away in a Manger /
Christmas Animals**

Puzzle Answers

page 53 · Three Kings

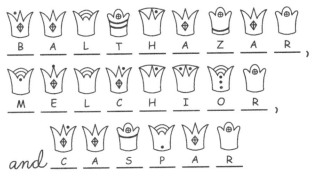

B A L T H A Z A R ,

M E L C H I O R ,

and C A S P A R

G O L D , M Y R R H , and

F R A N K I N C E N S E

page 56 · Where's the Star?

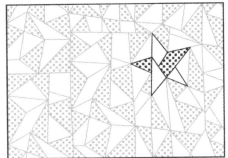

page 54–55 · Good Tidings of Great Joy

page 56 · Christmas Story

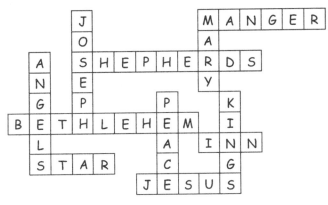

Puzzle Answers

page 57 · Advent Calendar

AND Day 1	**SET** Day 2	**ELL** Day 3	**PRE** Day 4
CANDLE	POINSETTIA	BELLS	PRESENT
NAM Day 5	**IGH** Day 6	**LAM** Day 7	**NDY** Day 8
ORNAMENT	SLEIGH	LAMB	CANDY CANE
ORN Day 9	**HOL** Day 10	**CRA** Day 11	**WFL** Day 12
HORN	HOLLY	NUTCRACKER	SNOWFLAKE
OOK Day 13	**RCH** Day 14	**BIR** Day 15	**REA** Day 16
COOKIE	CHURCH	BIRD	WREATH
TOC Day 17	**MEL** Day 18	**CRO** Day 19	**ROL** Day 20
STOCKING	CAMEL	CROWN	CAROL
DRU Day 21	**STA** Day 22	**NGE** Day 23	**TIV** Day 24
DRUM	STAR	ANGEL	NATIVITY

page 58 · Circular Symbol / Holy Time

CANDLES
symbolize
HOPE
OℇPH

EVERGREEN
symbolizes
NEW LIFE
ℇWN ℇILF

CIRCLE
symbolizes
ETERNITY
YNTℇℇRIT

page 59 · Angel Voices

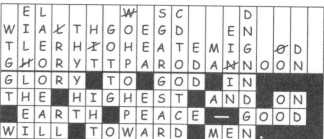

G	L	O	R	Y		T	O		G	O	D		I	N	
T	H	E		H	I	G	H	E	S	T		A	N	D		O	N
	E	A	R	T	H		P	E	A	C	E		—		G	O	O	D
W	I	L	L		T	O	W	A	R	D		M	E	N	.

Halo, there!

page 60 · Holy Place

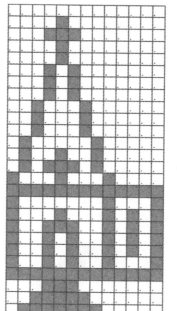

page 60 · Joyful Noise

JOY TO THE WORLD

124

Puzzle Answers

page 62 · **Reindeer Games**

E A D N C R = D A N C E R *Extra fun:*
P U I C D = C U P I D Vixen is the
R E N N O D = D O N N E R missing
E O C M T = C O M E T reindeer.
E T I B N Z L = B L I T Z E N
E R N R P A C = P R A N C E R
R H A D S E = D A S H E R

page 62 · **Cool Cash**

A. Opposite of yes

$\underset{2}{N}\ \underset{6}{O}$

B. To forbid something

$\underset{8}{B}\ \underset{3}{A}\ \underset{5}{N}$

C. Opposite of lose

$\underset{7}{W}\ \underset{1}{I}\ \underset{10}{N}$

D. Make a request

$\underset{9}{A}\ \underset{4}{S}\ \underset{11}{K}$

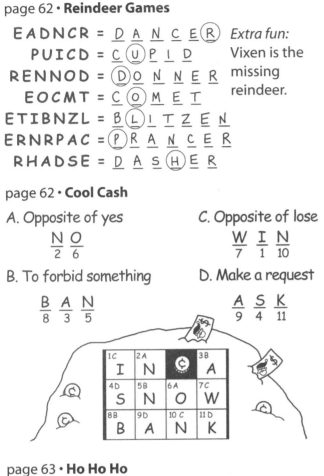

1 C	2 A		3 B
I	N	C	A
4 D	5 B	6 A	7 C
S	N	O	W
8 B	9 D	10 C	11 D
B	A	N	K

page 63 · **Ho Ho Ho**

5 Brrrr-itos!

7 Chimney-changas!

8 Because snow would melt in Africa!

3 A F-rose!

1 North Polish!

6 A flake rake!

2 Rude-olph!

9 The glove compartment!

4 Elf S. Presley!

page 63 · **Rolling Riddle**
Santa rolling down the hill!

page 64 · **Crazy Train**

page 65 · **Go See Santa**

Puzzle Answers

page 66 · Fatten Him Up

```
              L P                W
        G     C A U              I
C   R   H R D F       P D        I
H E ' S H U G G A B L E          P D
U A     E B E Y T U U            U U
N T     F B     Y T   L M        L M
K O     T Y           K P        K P
Y U     Y                        Y
  T
```

page 66 · Mrs. Claus's Cooking

To figure out how many servings of stew an elf had, count the number of dark stripes on his hat! The elves ate 28 total servings of stew.

page 67 · Sad Santa, Glad Santa

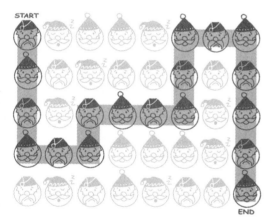

page 67 · All Gone!

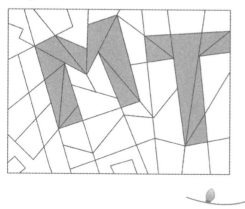

page 68 · Silly Santa

H O L <u>E</u> = the opening in a chimney

H O <u>T</u> <u>E</u> L = place where travelers pay to sleep

H O <u>S</u> E = rubber tube that squirts water

H O <u>M</u> E = place where a person lives

H O L <u>Y</u> = sacred or religious

H O <u>L</u> <u>D</u> = keep in a certain position

H O <u>A</u> <u>X</u> = story meant to fool people

H O <u>P</u> E = wish for something

page 68 · Santaspeak

To translate a message into Santaspeak, you must add H-O after every letter. When you cross out all the extra HOs, the riddle reads, "What's yellow and goes "ho ho ho"? Santa Banana!

page 68 · Twin Santas?

page 69 · Jingle Yells

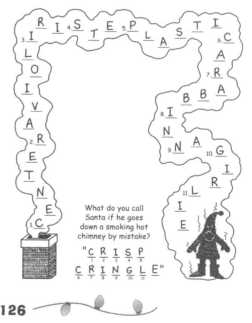

What do you call Santa if he goes down a smoking hot chimney by mistake?

"<u>C</u> <u>R</u> <u>I</u> <u>S</u> <u>P</u>
_{1 2 3 4 5}
<u>C</u> <u>R</u> <u>I</u> <u>N</u> <u>G</u> <u>L</u> <u>E</u>"
_{6 7 8 9 10 11}

Puzzle Answers

page 70 · **Checking It Twice**

Naughty

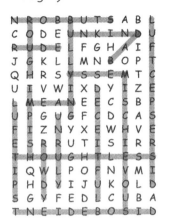

Nice

```
N R O B B U T S A B L
C O D E U N K I N D U
R U D E L F G H A I F
J G K L L M N B O P T
Q H R S Y S S E M T C
U I V W I X D Y I Z E
L M E A N E E C S B P
U P G U G F C D C A S
F I Z N Y X E W H V E
E S R R U T I S I R R
T H O U G H T L E S S
I Q W L P O F N V M I
P H D Y I J U K O L D
S G Y F E D L C U B A
T N E I D E B O S I D
```

```
O B E D I E N T S I F
E L B A E E R G A L E
A J N R Y I J V U O D
N E A T Z C X F R Y W
B K E S A H T R Q A E
H L T R G H I G P L H
C E T G F U E O H C G
D N U E L N E G O O N
G M O P D E H D N N M
E H P U F T F L M I I
T O O V E U U Y D V N
F N P E C B N L O G E
G E W W A Z I U K L C
H G Q X Y K W T J G B
I T E L B A I L E R A
```

page 71 · **Letter to Santa**

E3Q4 WQH5Q,
DEAR SANTA,
8 YQF3 G33H F346 T99E 5Y8W 63Q4.
I HAVE BEEN VERY GOOD THIS YEAR.
0O3QW3 G48HT J3 Q 0Q8H5 W35,
PLEASE BRING ME A PAINT SET,
Q 5303WD903, QHE Q 43QOO6 T99E
A TELESCOPE, AND A REALLY GOOD
G99I. 5YQHI 697 F346 J7DY.
BOOK. THANK YOU VERY MUCH.
6974 R483HE, JQ48WWQ
YOUR FRIEND, MARISSA
0.W. YQF3 Q WQR3 5480!
P.S. HAVE A SAFE TRIP!

page 72 · **Scrambled Sleigh**

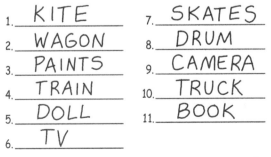

1. KITE
2. WAGON
3. PAINTS
4. TRAIN
5. DOLL
6. TV
7. SKATES
8. DRUM
9. CAMERA
10. TRUCK
11. BOOK

page 74 · **Holiday Hink Pinks**

What do you call...

...an evergreen that costs nothing?
F R E E
T R E E

...a really nice ringing decoration?
S W E L L
B E L L

...a really fast Santa?
Q U I C K
N I C K

...moving slowly through a crowded shopping center?
M A L L
C R A W L

...a not-short Christmas carol?
L O N G
S O N G

page 74 · **What a Pal!**

P A L A C E
fancy home for a king

P A L E
not bright in color

P A L E T T E
a board on which artists mix colors

P A L A M I N O
a golden-colored horse

P A L M
inside surface of the hand

P A L L E T
mattress made of straw

P A L I N D R O M E
word that is the same backwards or forwards

page 75 · **Box It Up**

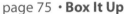

page 75 · **Waiting Game**

Dan is first in line, Charlie is second, Drew is third, and Chris is last.

Puzzle Answers

page 76 · **Stuck on Stamps**

page 76 ·

Christmas Letter

The code is simple — the last letter of each word is moved to the front! Here's how the letter should read:

DECEMBER 2003

DEAR FRIENDS,

WE HAVE BEEN VERY BUSY THIS YEAR!

BOB GOT A NEW JOB AND WE MOVED TO NEW JERSEY.

MARY WROTE A NEW BOOK WHICH IS SELLING WELL.

TOM IS LEARNING TO PLAY THE TRUMPET, AND SARAH JOINED THE GIRL SCOUTS.

EW WENT TO FLORIDA ON VACATION AND HAD A GOOD TIME.

WE ARE ALL WELL.
HOPE YOU ARE, TOO!

LOVE,

BOB, MARY, TOM, AND SARAH

page 77 · **Address Unknown**

page 78 · **All Around Town**

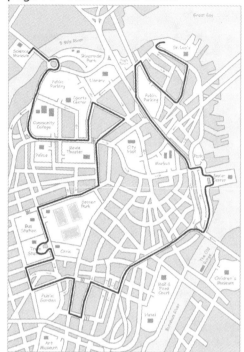

page 79 · **Here We Go A-Caroling**

DECK THE HALLS

Missing Letters = D, L, O, T

DECK THE HALLS WITH BOUGHS OF HOLLY, FA, LA, LA, LA, LA, LA, LA, LA, LA.

AWAY IN A MANGER

Missing Letters = A, B, S, T

AWAY IN A MANGER, NO CRIB FOR A BED. THE LITTLE LORD JESUS LAID DOWN HIS SWEET HEAD.

Puzzle Answers

page 79 · **Here We Go A-Caroling** *continued*

JINGLE BELLS

Missing Letters: B, N, H, S

JI**N**GLE **B**ELL**S**, JI**N**GLE **B**ELL**S**,

JI**N**GLE ALL T**H**E WAY. O**H**,

W**H**AT FU**N** IT I**S** TO RIDE I**N**

A O**N**E **H**OR**S**E, OPE**N** **S**LEIG**H**.

O COME ALL YE FAITHFUL

Missing Letters = E, C, F, H

O **C**OM**E** ALL Y**E** **F**AIT**H F**UL,

JOY**F**UL AND TRIUMP**H**ANT.

O **C**OM**E** Y**E**, O **C**OM**E**

Y**E**, TO B**E**THL**E H E**M.

page 79 · **Crazy Caroler**

18 rectangles, 17 circles, 7 ovals, and 15 triangles

page 80 · **Family Photos**

page 81 · **The More, the Merrier**

energy	region(s)	sir	tie(s)
get	rent(s)	sire	tin
gone	rest	sit	tine(s)
got	rig(s)	site	tire(s)
green,	ring(s)	snore	toe(s)
greet(s)	rise,	snort,	ton
grit	rite(s)	sore	tone
in	rose	sort	toner
is	rosy	soy	tore
it	rote	sting	torn,
no	see	stingy	toy(s)
nose	seen	stone	try
note(s)	sent	story	yen
one	sing	ten	yet
on	singe	tenor(s)	

page 81 · **'Tis the Season**

The connection between all the items listed in the puzzle is that they all are things that can be given.

Puzzle Answers

page 82 • People Helping People

Small wagon - T + Jewelry on a finger = <u>CARING</u>

Opposite of bad + Opposite of won't = <u>GOODWILL</u>

First half of charcoal + Second half of purity = <u>CHARITY</u>

First half of helpless + Opposite of empty – L = <u>HELPFUL</u>

Instrument that points north + Roaring animal – L = <u>COMPASSION</u>

First half of symbol + Small trail + Y = <u>SYMPATHY</u>

page 82 • Christmas Baskets

Mittens ♡♡	226	622
Toothbrushes	1734	7431
Teddy Bears	19	91
Hats	154	541
Canned Food	4257	7542
Frozen Turkeys	428	842

page 83 • Secret Santas

	Gives To	Receives From
Tonya	KRYSTAL	MATT
Ethan	MIGUEL	MIGUEL
Matt	TONYA	KATE
Miguel	ETHAN	ETHAN
Kate	MATT	KRYSTAL
Krystal	KATE	TONYA

page 84 • Toys for Tots

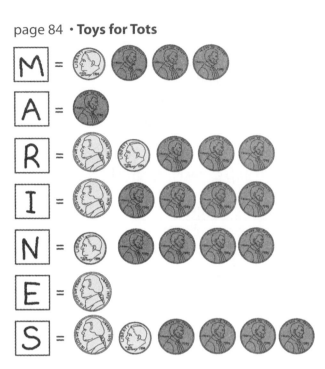

page 86 • Party Date

Puzzle Answers

page 86 • Luke's List

EXTRA FUN: It seems Luke was also thinking about Easter, 4th of July, and Halloween as he made up his Christmas party list!

~~corn-on-the-cob~~
~~candy corn~~
popcorn balls
~~iced tea~~
ice skates
~~ice cream cones~~

~~American flag~~
"Santa Stops Here" flag
~~pumpkin~~
~~tombstone~~
tree stand
~~cider~~
~~lemonade~~
~~sparklers~~
colored lights
~~flashlights~~
hot chocolate
~~chocolate bunny~~
candy canes
~~jelly beans~~
~~scary mask~~

white beard
~~rotten eggs~~
eggnog
~~plastic eggs~~
firewood
~~firecrackers~~
marshmallows
~~marshmallow chicks~~
~~hotdogs~~
turkey
tinsel
~~cobwebs~~
stockings
~~baskets~~
~~red / blue balloons~~
red / green balloons

page 89 • Fractional Feast

page 87 • By the Numbers

page 88 • Party Prep

1. Set a date on your calendar.
2. Choose your guests and send invites.
3. Make a shopping list for supplies.
4. Get the groceries and party favors.
5. Clean the whole house very well.
6. Decorate and set the party table.

page 90 • Eggnog, Anyone?

```
G G E O G E E G E E
G E G N E G G E G G
E G G N G O G N G E
N G G G E O N E N G
G O N G O N G G E G
G N O E G G N O O N
E G G N O N G G E O
```

page 90 • Cookie Filling

page 90 • Pass the Bubbly

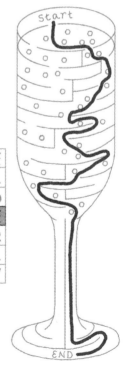

Puzzle Answers

page 91 · Sing-Along

THE (1) (L)	(The First Noel)
FROS T THE [snowman]	(Frosty the Snowman)
O [caroler] [sky]	(O Holy Night)
[person] [sky]	(Silent Night)
JING L [bell]	(Jingle Bells)
[window] VER [bell]	(Silver Bells)
[eye] [saw] [ship]	(I Saw Three Ships)
O [tree]	(O Christmas Tree)

page 92 · Pin the _____ on the _____ ?

1. Pin the __STAR__ on the __TREE__.
2. Pin the __BOW__ on the __PRESENT__.
3. Pin the __EARS__ on the __ELF__.
4. Pin the __BEARD__ on the __SANTA__.
5. Pin the __ANTLERS__ on the __REINDEER__.
6. Pin the __WREATH__ on the __DOOR__.

page 92 · Thanks for Inviting Me

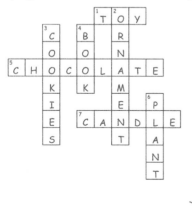

page 93 · Santa Ring Toss

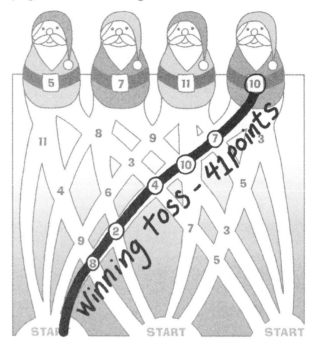

Winning toss – 41 points

page 94 · Grab Bag

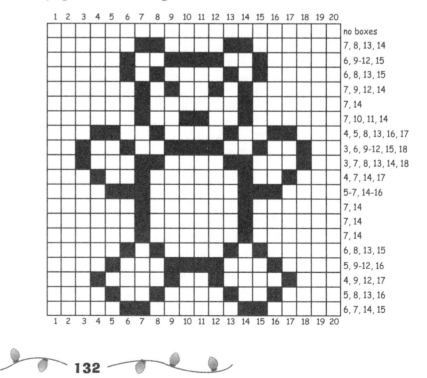

	no boxes
	7, 8, 13, 14
	6, 9-12, 15
	6, 8, 13, 15
	7, 9, 12, 14
	7, 14
	7, 10, 11, 14
	4, 5, 8, 13, 16, 17
	3, 6, 9-12, 15, 18
	3, 7, 8, 13, 14, 18
	4, 7, 14, 17
	5-7, 14-16
	7, 14
	7, 14
	7, 14
	6, 8, 13, 15
	5, 9-12, 16
	4, 9, 12, 17
	5, 8, 13, 16
	6, 7, 14, 15

Puzzle Answers

page 95 · **Where's the Party?**

Party starts here at 7 o'clock.

HID
THIS
~~DOCK~~
IS
~~PLACED~~
~~HOPPY~~
THE
~~PROP~~
~~PUPPY~~
PLACE
~~PRANK~~

~~BRIM~~
~~GUPPY~~
BETTER
~~BATTED~~
LUCK
~~BOXED~~
NEXT
~~SOCK~~
TIME
~~ZIPPY~~

~~BED~~
~~HAPPY~~
SORRY
~~PRY~~
TRY
~~PROB~~
AGAIN
~~ROCK~~
~~TRIED~~

page 96 · **And to All, a Good Night**

really nice, really good, really magical

Christmas

page 98 · **Christmas Characters**

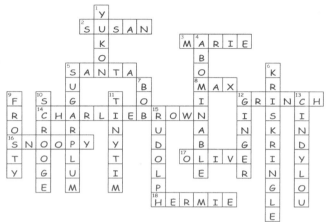

page 99 · **Story Starter**

~~SO~~	(A)	~~SLEIGH~~	~~ON~~	~~TOP~~
~~CANDY~~	~~DROP~~	~~OR~~	(VISIT)	~~BED~~
~~CHOP~~	~~SLOW~~	~~CAROL~~	~~RED~~	~~HEAR~~
~~BED~~	~~GO~~	(FROM)	~~TO~~	~~CHIMNEY~~
~~CHRIST~~	~~HOP~~	~~NEAR~~	~~SLIP~~	~~CARDS~~
~~NO~~	(SAINT)	~~PEER~~	~~STOP~~	~~HEED~~
~~CHURCH~~	~~LEO~~	(NICHOLAS)	~~YEAR~~	~~REAR~~

page 99 · **Dancing Story**

O	F	A	I	T	P	A	S	R	C
N	U	T	C	R	A	C	K	E	R
E	N	E	E	Y	T	E	I	D	Y

page 100 · **Perfect Present**
Each person's artwork will be different!

page 100 · **Christmas Classic**

A CHRISTMAS CAROL BY CHARLES DICKENS

Puzzle Answers

page 101 • Bulging Bookcase

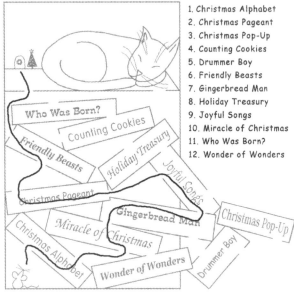

1. Christmas Alphabet
2. Christmas Pageant
3. Christmas Pop-Up
4. Counting Cookies
5. Drummer Boy
6. Friendly Beasts
7. Gingerbread Man
8. Holiday Treasury
9. Joyful Songs
10. Miracle of Christmas
11. Who Was Born?
12. Wonder of Wonders

page 103 • Scary Christmas?

1 A	2 D	3 E		4 A	5 B	6 E	7 C			
T	H	E		K	I	N	G			
8 C	9 C		10 E	11 B	12 E		13 D	14 A	15 A	16 D
O	F		T	H	E		M	I	C	E

A. Sound a clock makes
T I C K
1 14 15 4

B. Short form of hello
H I
11 5

C. Cloud close to the ground
F O G
9 8 7

D. Border of a piece of cloth
H E M
2 16 13

E. Person aged 13 to 19
T E E N
10 3 12 6

page 103 • Not Your Average Mouse

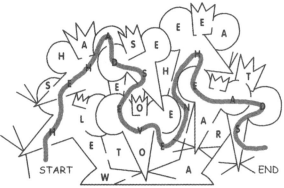

START   END

Answer: He had seven heads!

page 102 • The Christmas Crazies

It was Christmas morning. __KELLY__ (name #1), __MAX__ (name #2)

and __NAT__ (name #3) came __SWIMMING__ (verb ending in "ing") down the

stairs. They started __TICKLING__ (a different verb ending in "ing") their gifts.

"__HUBBA HUBBA__ (exclamation)!" said __KELLY__ (name #1). "I got a

__PINK__ (color) __PENCIL__ (thing #1)." "__GNARLY__ (a different exclamation)!" said

__MAX__ (name #2). "I love this __ORANGE__ (adjective) __SLIPPER__ (thing #2)."

"__AWESOME__ (a different exclamation)!" said __NAT__ (name #3). "I've always

wanted a __SOFA__ (thing #3)." Just then, Mom and Dad came

__HOPPING__ (a different verb ending in "ing") into the room.

"Merry __ST. PATRICK'S DAY__ (name of a holiday)!" they said. "Time for

__DINNER__ (a meal). Anybody want some __CUCUMBER__ (kind of food)?"

"Merry __GROUNDHOG DAY__ (name of another holiday) to you, too!" said

__KELLY__ (name #1) and __MAX__ (name #2). "Let's eat!"

"__OH BOY__ (a different exclamation)!" yelled __NAT__ (name #3),

"Then we can all __FLY KITES__ (activity) together!"

Everyone's answer will be completely different and crazy! However, here is a look at our answer in case you're curious.

page 104 • Nutty Nutcrackers

134

Puzzle Answers

page 105 · **The Little Drummer Boy**

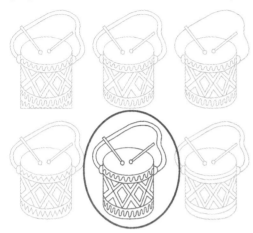

page 106 · **Picture This**

page 106–107 ·
**Not a Creature
Was Stirring . . .**

page 108 ·
**Santa's
Goodbye**

MERRY CHRISTMAS TO ALL,

THE EVERYTHING® KIDS' SERIES!

Packed with tons of information, activities, and puzzles, the Everything® Kids' books are perennial bestsellers that keep kids active and engaged. Each book is 8" x 9¼", 144 pages, and two-color throughout.

All this at the incredible price of $6.95!

The Everything® Kids' Knock
Knock Book
1-59337-127-6

The Everything® Kids' Hidden
Pictures Book
1-59337-128-4

The Everything® Kids' Baseball Book, 3rd Ed.
  1-59337-070-9

The Everything® Kids' Bible Trivia Book
  1-59337-031-8

The Everything® Kids' Bugs Book
  1-58062-892-3

The Everything® Kids' Christmas Puzzle &
  Activity Book
  1-58062-965-2

The Everything® Kids' Cookbook
  1-58062-658-0

The Everything® Kids' Halloween Puzzle &
  Activity Book
  1-58062-959-8

The Everything® Kids' Joke Book
  1-58062-686-6

The Everything® Kids' Math Puzzles Book
  1-58062-773-0

The Everything® Kids' Mazes Book
  1-58062-558-4

The Everything® Kids' Money Book
  1-58062-685-8

The Everything® Kids' Monsters Book
  1-58062-657-2

The Everything® Kids' Nature Book
  1-58062-684-X

The Everything® Kids' Puzzle Book
  1-58062-687-4

The Everything® Kids' Riddles & Brain Teasers Book
  1-59337-036-9

The Everything® Kids' Science Experiments Book
  1-58062-557-6

The Everything® Kids' Soccer Book
  1-58062-642-4

The Everything® Kids' Travel Activity Book
  1-58062-641-6

Trade Paperback, $14.95
1-58062-147-3, 304 pages

The Everything® Bedtime Story Book

by Mark Binder

The Everything® Bedtime Story Book is a wonderfully original collection of 100 stories that will delight the entire family. Accompanied by charming illustrations, the stories included are retold in an exceptionally amusing style and are perfect for reading aloud. From familiar nursery rhymes to condensed American classics, this collection promises to promote sweet dreams, active imaginations, and quality family time.

Trade Paperback, $12.95
1-58062-546-0, 304 pages

The Everything® Fairy Tales Book

by Amy Peters

Take your children to magical lands where animals talk, mythical creatures wander freely, and good and evil come in every imaginable form. You'll find all this and more in *The Everything® Fairy Tales Book*, an extensive collection of 100 classic fairy tales. This enchanting compilation features charming, original illustrations that guarantee creative imaginations and quality family time.

Available wherever books are sold!
To order, call 800-872-5627 or visit us at www.*everything*.com